Faith and Freedom

Faith and Freedom

Teresa Forcades

polity

First published in 2017 by Polity Press

Polity Press
65 Bridge Street
Cambridge CB2 1UR, UK

Polity Press
350 Main Street
Malden, MA 02148, USA

ISBN-13: 978-1-5095-0975-1
ISBN-13: 978-1-5095-0976-8(pb)

A catalogue record for this book is available from the British Library.

Library of Congress Cataloging-in-Publication Data

Names: Forcades i Vila, Teresa, author.
Title: Faith and freedom / Teresa Forcades.
Description: Malden, MA : Polity, 2016. | Includes bibliographical references.
Identifiers: LCCN 2016016612 (print) | LCCN 2016031510 (ebook) |
ISBN 9781509509751 (hardback) | ISBN 9781509509768 (pbk.) |
ISBN 9781509509782 (Mobi) | ISBN 9781509509799 (Epub)
Subjects: LCSH: Catholic Church–Doctrines–Meditations.
Classification: LCC BX2182.3 .F67 2016 (print) | LCC BX2182.3 (ebook) |
DDC 230/.2–dc23
LC record available at https://lccn.loc.gov/2016016612
Typeset in 12.5 on 15 pt Adobe Garamond
by Toppan Best-set Premedia Limited
Printed and bound in the United Kingdom by Clays Ltd, St Ives PLC

For further information on Polity, visit our website: politybooks.com

Contents

CONTENTS

Introduction

Life as a Benedictine nun has been both a gift and a challenge ever since I entered the monastery eighteen years ago. I have enjoyed the beauty and the freedom of prayer, and have also encountered personal hardships in our earnest community life. I have known periods of dry or even anguished prayer, and have experienced the joy of being lifted up by my sisters' wit.

After studying science, and becoming a medical doctor, I went on to study feminist theology in the United States before entering the monastery at the age of thirty-one. Nine years later, in 2006, having completed a doctorate in Public Health and being close to finishing a doctorate in Fundamental Theology, I wrote a report on the crimes of big pharmaceutical companies. I soon became well-known in my own country as a denouncer of medical abuses and an advocate for women's and LGBT rights in the Roman Catholic Church. Wider popularity came in 2009 with an hour-long internet video that exposed the gap between public policy and scientific evidence with regard to the swine-flu vaccine. The video had more than one million hits and I was flooded with encouraging emails. Soon afterwards, in the context of the growing economic crisis, I began to come under pressure to engage politically. In April 2013, together with the Catalan economist Arcadi Oliveres and about forty other social and political activists, I was involved in setting up a political movement, called Procés Constituent, which stands for an independent and anti-capitalist Catalonia. In June 2015, with monastic permission, I took leave of my community temporarily in order to engage in active politics for a maximum of three years.

The book you are about to read is the first I have written directly in English. It brings together my thoughts on the issues most fundamental

to me: freedom and love, social justice and political engagement, public health, feminism, faith
and forgiveness. It is divided into six chapters
named after the five canonical hours that
give the monastic day its peculiar rhythm
(matins, lauds, sext, vespers, and compline), plus
the hour of *recreation*, the daily gathering of the
community.

1 Matins: love and freedom

It's pitch black in Montserrat. Quiet. Down below the mountain, the serpentine yellow lights of the village of Monistrol. Above, bright stars. The bell rings at 6 a.m. and at 6:30 the first prayer of the day starts: matins. Half asleep, braced against the winter cold, we gather in the monastery church and face the large window above the altar with its serene Christ on the Cross. It is a simple piece of unpainted clay in the style of the old Romanesque *Maiestas*. Jesus reflects no pain and hangs effortlessly, as if ready to fly from the cross, as if he had nothing to do with such gruesome torture. His arms are not aligned but stretch forward in an open embrace:

4

the cross hangs in the middle of a large corner window with a panoramic view of the mountains, and the arms have to accommodate themselves to the square angle left by the tall brick walls. At this dark hour, the window glass reflects the hanging Christ and duplicates his embrace, redirecting it towards the wider world outside the church walls.

"And the curtain of the temple was torn in two, from top to bottom." This is how the Gospel of Mark explains the consequences of Jesus' death (Mark 15:38). The reference is to the temple that stood in Jerusalem in the first century CE: its curtain isolated the space where God dwelt, which could only be entered by the high priest at strictly prescribed times. Mark wants to make clear that Jesus had nothing to do with such separation and regulation. Jesus came precisely to free God from such ungodly constraints. Jesus' name *Emmanuel* means "God with us." God with us, God among us. The Spanish mystic Teresa of Ávila put it even more plainly: *Entre pucheros anda el Señor* (God walks amidst the kitchen pots).

No organ is played during the matins prayer, and there is almost no singing except on Sundays or major festivities. Voices are still hoarse from sleep, so reciting rather than singing the psalms helps warm them up for the next prayer, the joyful lauds. Matins is sober. It is also called the "office of readings": its distinctive feature consists of two relatively long readings (around two pages each) proclaimed from the lectern. The first is from the Bible, the second from classical theological treatises, most of them belonging to the first centuries of Christianity, the so-called "patristic era." Patristic theology, despite being more than 1,500 years old, has not lost its power to speak to the heart; this is because it was written at a time when Christian believers had no social standing at all and were considered a bunch of ignorant peasants or in some cases a dangerous fanatical sect. Some of those early Christians refused to acknowledge the divine status of the Roman Emperor and were sentenced to death for doing so. Not all were heroes, though. Quite a few, probably the majority, gave up in the face of persecution and tried to dilute the message handed down by Jesus, to make it less sharp and uncomfortable. Clear injunctions to social upheaval such as: "You know that among the nations those whom they recognize as their rulers lord it over them, and their great ones are tyrants over them; but it should not be so among you" (Mark 10:42) coexisted at that time with open endorsements of the status quo: "Slaves, accept the authority of your masters with all deference, not only those who are kind and gentle but also those who are harsh" (1 Peter 2:12). These contradictions coexisted then and continue to coexist today, for both these sentences can be found in the New Testament.

Often, while listening to a biblical or patristic text during matins, I am elated or deeply moved. At other times, I am frustrated or even angered. On a couple of occasions when I have been the reader I have omitted a sentence of the text because I found it too offensive; for example: "I permit no woman to teach or to have authority over a man; she is to keep silent" (1 Timothy 2:12). On these occasions, I think of Howard Thurman's grandmother. Thurman was one of the greatest African-American philosophers and theologians of the twentieth century, a friend of Mahatma Gandhi and a mentor to Martin Luther King Jr. Thurman's grandmother had been a slave most of her life. She was an illiterate deeply devout Christian who forbade her

7

grandson to ever read to her from the letters of Paul because she knew that they contained the statement: "Slaves, be obedient to your earthly masters with fear and trembling, in singleness of heart, as you obey Christ" (Ephesians 6:5). She refused to acknowledge this as the word of God.

This is what the matins prayer with its long biblical readings invites me to do: to take personal responsibility for my own faith. I do not have faith in a book. I honor the Bible and cannot imagine my life without it. I read from it every day (or almost every day), but I do not expect the text of the Bible to hinder my thinking, or be a substitute for it. I do believe that the text – the different texts – of the Bible are inspired by God and, precisely because of that, they do not collide with my freedom but count on it. God – such has been my experience – has never collided with my freedom; She has created the space where my freedom can exist and invites me to own it. God has never invited me to give up my freedom in order to obey or to please Her. God takes no pleasure in slaves: "I do not call you servants any longer, because the servant does not know what the master is doing; but I have called you friends" (John 15:15).

God takes no pleasure in slaves but enjoys friendship and freedom. The first book of theology I ever read was Leonardo Boff's *Jesus the Liberator*. I was fifteen years old at the time, and part of a family that mistrusted the Roman Catholic Church despite having had me and my two sisters baptized into it. The three of us were born during the dictatorship of General Francisco Franco, who imposed a fascist regime known as "National Catholicism," religiously sanctioned by the hierarchy of the Spanish Catholic Church. My parents opposed Franco and resented the support that the Church gave to his regime. I read *Jesus the Liberator* because I was eager to learn more about Jesus after being shaken to the core by reading the gospels for the first time. I remember being deeply affected, but I don't remember having felt "personally liberated" by God: this first religious experience of mine had more to do with making sense of life than with liberation. As a teenager, I didn't feel oppressed; I was rather content and full of plans. It was only much later, while studying theology in the Unites States in the 1990s, that I came across the text of the Enuma Elish and realized, at least at a theoretical level, how seriously the biblical God takes human freedom and how deeply involved She is in supporting it.

The Enuma Elish is the ancient Babylonian Creation narrative that directly inspired the biblical book of Genesis. Its name means "when above" and reflects the opening words of the text: "when the sky above was not named and the earth beneath did not yet bear a name..." This epic poem of about 1,000 lines was first discovered in 1848 among the archeological remains of Ashurbanipal's library in Nineveh (present-day Mosul, in Iraq). The clay tablets of Nineveh are fragmentary and were written in Akkadian cuneiform script in the seventh century BCE. New tablets of the same text were discovered in Assur (Iraq) in the twentieth century; these had been written in Assyrian in the tenth century BCE. The original Enuma Elish is presumed to have been written in the eighteenth century BCE in Babylon during the Hammurabi dynasty. Its narrative dominated Mesopotamian cosmogonies for more than 1,000 years and greatly influenced those of its Near Eastern neighbors. The Enuma Elish includes what seems to be the most ancient notion of a creator God (Marduk), who shapes the world in seven days with a distinct order that resembles evolution: it starts with the planet (the separation of heaven and earth) and ends with human life.

In the sixth century BCE, the Israelites lost a major war against the Chaldean king Nebuchadnezzar. Jerusalem was destroyed and the Hebrew elites were deported to Babylon where they were greatly impressed by their captors' magnificent capital city and by its cultural and religious achievements. The majority of them abandoned their Hebrew tradition and embraced that of the victorious Babylonians – the majority, but not all. Some Hebrews sensed in their defeated provincial tradition a value superior to the wealth and splendor of the imperial city and took up the task of writing a cosmogony, a narrative of Creation, which dared to contradict the venerable Enuma Elish on some crucial points. The most fundamental of these departures from the original text was their depiction of the existential predicament of the human being vis-à-vis God. According to the Enuma Elish, God, having created the world, rests on the seventh day and commands humans to serve Her. According to the biblical Genesis, God, having created the world, rests on the seventh day and invites humans and all of Creation to rest along with Her. The purpose of human life according to the Babylonians was to serve God, to fulfill God's (or God's representatives') needs; according to the Israelites, on the contrary, the purpose of human life is to enter into a personal friendship with God. The human being of the Babylonian Creation is instrumental: her goal is to fulfill God. The human being of the biblical Creation is free: her goal is to fulfill herself.

As the biblical quotes at the beginning of this chapter illustrate, this most fundamental faith in human radical freedom and its biblical corollary (friendship with God as the goal of human life) has tended to get lost in the historical development of religious institutions and of religious consciousness. Even in the Bible itself, there are many instances where Yahweh (the biblical God) acts as the Babylonian Marduk, using humans for Her own purposes and blatantly ignoring their fundamental freedom. A most notable case is the episode of the drowning of the Egyptians in the Red Sea: in order to liberate the Israelites, God kills the Egyptians (Exodus 14:20–31). It is difficult to see how Yahweh respects the fundamental freedom of the Egyptians here. Paradoxically, this episode – which is so problematic for contemporary consciousness to interpret positively, since God kills some people in order to favor others – seems nevertheless to dramatize the core historical experience of the ancient Israelites: God's liberation of them from slavery. We don't know what really happened in history, but we do know what the Israelites believed and wrote about themselves: we were slaves in Egypt and God took pity on us and made us free – not because we were any better than the Egyptians, but because we were oppressed and we suffered.

The biblical reading of matins is over, now comes the patristic. The second reading today is from Gregory, the fourth-century bishop of Nazianz (in modern Turkey). Gregory defended his Christian understanding of freedom against the dominant view of his time as daringly and as vehemently as the ancient Israelites had done ten centuries earlier. It is clear that neither the exiled Israelites nor Bishop Gregory and the other fathers and mothers of the Church had notions of personal freedom comparable to those of our twenty-first century; the individual subject of modernity with his claims to autonomy had not yet developed. But, arguably, they had that without which the subject of modernity would have never developed at all – a deep personal experience that gave them the courage to defend against all odds, in a sharp and consistent way, the idea of a radically free relationship between the human being and God. Taking this into account, modernity can be described as developing simultaneously both *against* and *from* historical Judaism and Christianity: *against* the social control exerted by ecclesiastical institutions and the submission of the individual consciousness to imposed articles of faith; *from* the radical freedom and dignity of the human being created in the image of God and called to friendship with Her.

Gregory of Nazianz challenged some of the fundamental ideas of Neoplatonism, the philosophy developed one century earlier by Plotinus which had become the dominant view amongst the cultural elites in Gregory's time. Plotinus held that the world came into existence through "spontaneous emanation" as an extension of God's self. Gregory categorically refused the notion of "emanation" and mockingly compared the Neoplatonic "emanating God" to a "spilling boiling pot." He contrasted this with the Christian notion of Creation as implying a free act on the part of God: an act that enables the world to be *other* than God.

There is a tendency today in Christian theology to argue along lines that sometimes mirror the Neoplatonic notion of emanation, in an attempt to overcome the sharp divide between God and the world that seems to be entailed by the patristic notion of "Creation." Thus, for example, the feminist theologian Sally McFague complements the traditional metaphor of the creator God as an artist (intellectual creation) with that of the creator God as a mother giving birth, highlighting that what is being born is not "a part" of the mother but a different reality that, despite being *different* from her, is nevertheless organically bound to her in a way that a work of art would never be bound to the artist who creates it. Some contemporary theologians use the word *panentheism* to distinguish their perspective from traditional *pantheism*, that is, from the notion of a complete continuity or identity between God and the world (as in Spinoza's dictum: *Deus sive natura*, God or nature). As opposed to pantheism, panentheism does acknowledge a distinction between God and the world (nature/universe), but considers nevertheless that the world exists *within* God and cannot be separated from Her.

Gregory's view is more radical: God has been able to create – and uninterruptedly sustains – a reality that can truly confront Her, oppose Her, refuse to identify with Her. Not in absolute terms, but in the here and now of contingent historical reality. God is free and can create from nothing. Human beings are also free and can refuse their link to God. God abhors this refusal but nevertheless sustains it out of respect for love. Love, God's essence and the goal of human life, is impossible to conceive without freedom. The notion of a break, fracture, or rupture is fundamental here. God has created and sustains a "space" where things can happen that have nothing to do with God or God's will; this space is "the world"; this space is "history." It would be outrageous (and a logical contradiction) to attempt to bring abuse and a truly benevolent God into alignment. And yet, our world, our history, is full of abuse. There are only two basic answers to this: either the benevolent God does not exist, or She has created the possibility that things – many things – happen in the world and in history that have nothing to do with Her and are against Her will.

This notion of a "break" between God and the world/history is not so easy to accept. It seems more coherent to argue either that there is a God and all that exists is contained in Her, or that there is no God at all. Speaking of a God that does not contain everything seems contradictory, as if one is speaking of a minor God, a limited God, a God that does not really deserve to be called so. Classical theology – Jewish and Christian – has wrestled with this question and reached the conclusion that if there is a space where God is not, if somehow there is a limit in God, then this limit has to be self-given: God has limited Herself in order to make space for "real otherness" to exist.

The self-limitation of God was given a name by the sixteenth-century Jewish philosopher Isaac Luria: *tzimtzum* (צמצום). The notion of *tzimtzum* appeals to the absurdity of imagining Creation as an act of "expansion" by God: towards *what* should God – who by definition encompasses all – expand? There is no "space" beyond God where something "other than God" can be created, where something "other than God" can exist. Pantheism or panentheism seem inevitable if one's idea of God is to be philosophically sound. Isaac Luria was indeed a philosopher, but he was also a mystic, a cabalist; he had (like the exiled Israelites of the sixth century BCE and the patristic theologians of the fourth century CE) a personal experience of God that allowed him to discover the radicality of his human freedom. He felt an irreducibility in him, a real "otherness" in him, such that he was able to stand in front of God as an "other," and be called by God into free communion with Her – called by God, invited by God, but never forced. The notion of *tzimtzum* is neither pantheistic nor panentheistic; it does not consider Creation to be "a part" of God nor does it consider that God can be present in it without due invitation. Luria defends the true alterity of Creation and consequently the true freedom of the human being created in the image of God. Between God and the world there is a caesura: a break, not a continuity. A break that is wanted and sustained by God. A break that is a grace intended to make possible a communion (a true friendship) freely willed by both parties: God and the human being.

This free will to communion is what characterizes – in classical Christian theology – the inner life of God the Trinity. The triune God is not conceived as a lonely or solitary monad, but as a communion of three persons (traditionally named Father, Son, and Holy Spirit). Communion is the only type of relationship that deserves the name *spiritual* because it is a union that respects (and fosters) the irreducibility of the other. In Greek it is known as *perichorese*; the etymology of the word (*peri*: around; *coreo*: to make space) helps us to understand its meaning: communion is a love that instead of identifying with the loved one, "makes space" around her; it is a free union that does not weaken but actively fosters the alterity of the other person, a union that breathes and lets the other be herself. According to the Gospel of John, Jesus, right before being arrested, facing torture and execution, prays four times that his followers have among them the same communion, the same *perichorese*, the same unity that he has with his Father (John 17:11, 21, 22, 23).

There is no ritual, conceptual, or controlling separation between God and us, only the separation needed for (real) freedom and (real) love to be possible, only the separation that is already present in God's own self: true otherness conceived as a prerequisite for true communion.

According to the Lurian notion of *tzimtzum*, God has made possible the true otherness of Creation by an act of self-contraction (this is the literal meaning of the Hebrew צמצום: concentration or contraction): God restricts Herself – freely, joyfully – in order to make space for us, and then invites us to restrict ourselves – freely, joyfully – to invite Her back; friendship with God is the goal of human life and Creation is the setting that makes this communion possible.

Friendship with God as the goal of human freedom – what a strange idea! Isn't it a contradiction to speak about freedom, about radical freedom, and then give it a prescribed goal? Doesn't freedom imply precisely the right and the duty, flatly *the need*, to self-define one's own existential goals?

One of the authors most often featured in the readings of matins is Augustine of Hippo. Bishop

Augustine, like Bishop Gregory, lived in the first centuries of the common era, when Christianity was a marginal cult expanding mostly among the poor, the slaves, and women – expanding mostly among the least free in society. The young Augustine wanted nothing to do with it; he, like Gregory, attended the best universities of his time and became a well-trained rhetor, a professional in the art of speaking; he felt contempt for the rather poor communities of Christians and for their texts and their ideas about the world. Despite the pleadings and tears of his Christian mother Monica, Augustine was attracted by Manicheism and sought to make sense of the world's abuse and violence by postulating a cosmic fight between Light and Darkness, not unlike that depicted in so many contemporary films (the *Star Wars* series, for instance).

After his conversion to Christianity, Augustine moved definitively away from the Manichean worldview and encountered many dialectical adversaries, philosophers of his time ready to challenge the unusual views of the still marginal sect of the Christians. Augustine's controversies with Pelagius (fifth century CE) forced him to refine and nuance his own view of human freedom, leading him to draw a distinction between "free will" (*liberum arbitrium*) and "freedom" (*libertas*), which I believe can prove useful for our time. Augustine considered "free will" to be a necessary condition for "freedom": without the capacity to choose as one sees fit with no external constrictions, there can be no freedom. Granted. But there is more. Augustine went deeper and realized that there are constraints that are "internal," constraints that affect the will and curtail freedom from within. Consider a woman who, having been educated to not only tolerate but even to cooperate in her own abuse, "freely chooses" to educate her daughter along the same lines. Or a racist who "freely chooses" to refuse any relationship with those whom she has learned to hate. Are we ready in these cases to conclude that the abused mother and the racist are simply exerting their freedom in a way that disagrees with our own? Or is there something else at stake? For Augustine, the capacity to choose cannot simply be equated with freedom; for freedom to take place, one needs to choose not only with no external constraint, but with no internal constraint either.

For Augustine, choosing with no constraints whatsoever (external or internal) equates one's choice "to love," "to doing good," "to doing justice." For Augustine, only the just, good, loving person is free. Hence his most famous dictum: *Dilige et quod vis fac* (Love and do what you will).

The critical question, however, comes swiftly to the twenty-first-century reader: who decides what is loving, what is good, or what is just in any given case? Aren't different versions possible? My experience in bioethics and in politics has convinced me of the difficulties in determining how to proceed in order to implement concretely what is "good" and "just." In some challenging bioethical cases, it might not be possible for a full board of well-intentioned and highly trained professionals to reach agreement. Reality is complex.

Accepting Augustine's distinction between "free will" and "freedom" in the twenty-first century does not imply a return to a pre-modern paternalism that would grant some sort of properly qualified body the right to define for others what "good" and "just" concretely mean. Of course the law must do that to a certain extent, but the law should only intervene when there is clear harm to a third or non-consenting party. Violence or abuse between consenting adults, as in sadomasochism, cannot be outlawed. What Augustine's distinction can inspire today is not paternalism or legalism. It is rather a renewed sense of existential responsibility. Augustine can help us to become more, not less critical: critical of the self-contented delusion whereby we equate freedom with free choice, in order to spare ourselves the trouble of reflecting on the "good" and the "just."

Matins is over. The chapel is still cold as we exit in an orderly procession and each of us returns to her cell for half an hour of solitary prayer. It is 7 a.m.

2 Lauds: social justice

The half hour between matins and lauds passes very quickly. I usually meditate in my cell on the readings that will be proclaimed later in the daily Eucharist. But there was a time when I used this solitary prayer time quite differently. When I entered the monastery in 1997, and for a few years after that, I felt a need to go out after matins: out into nature, into the brisk morning air, to take in the wide horizon visible from our mountaintop. I still do it occasionally. I enjoy being outdoors and smelling the moist soil, surrounded at first by darkness and silence and then by a subtle light and sound imperceptibly increasing until the sun finally appears. I used to jump up and down quite vigorously to warm myself in the chilly winter air – so vigorously in fact that, a few months later, some of the nuns wondered what could have caused that hollow in our garden right at the spot where the village of Monistrol and the monastic cemetery, located on opposite slopes, can be seen simultaneously. While jumping, I watched alternately the village waking up to a new day and the cemetery, with the dead sisters reminding me that life is short.

The chapel is warmer at lauds and usually there are a few guests who share in our prayer; some are staying in our guesthouse, others drive up from the neighboring towns. The window with the hanging Christ above the altar is full of light now and prayer travels easily through it and beyond the monastic enclosure. "Come to me, all you that are weary and are carrying heavy burdens, and I will give you rest" (Matthew 11:28). The concern for social justice lies at the very heart of the Jewish and the Christian message. The ancient Israelites were slaves in Egypt and the biblical psalms – 150 beautiful ancient poems – bear witness to this, reminding all those who recite them that slavery is far from being over.

In September 2015, Oxfam International published a report entitled "A Europe for the many, not the few," denouncing the fact that today 123 million people in the European Union, almost a quarter of the EU population, live below the poverty line. Of those, 50 million live in plain misery, while the EU allows a level of tax avoidance and evasion worth an estimated 1 trillion euros annually that mostly favors big corporations. One trillion euros is five times the total amount invested in rescuing Greece and twice the amount invested in public health in the twenty-eight EU countries taken together. Eight and a half million European workers live in poverty despite having a full-time job, while the number of European multimillionaires increases. The divide between rich and poor grows alarmingly in Europe as in the rest of the world. In an earlier report from January 2015, "Wealth: Having it all and wanting more," Oxfam International had already denounced the widening gap between rich and poor: in 2010, 388 billionaires owned as much wealth as the bottom 50 percent of the world's population; by 2014, that figure had reduced to just 80 billionaires; in 2016, the report predicted, it will finally be true that 1 percent of the world's population will have accumulated more wealth than the remaining 99 percent.

"No one can serve two masters; for a slave will either hate the one and love the other, or be devoted to the one and despise the other. You cannot serve God and wealth" (Matthew 6:24). Those are Jesus' words, but the fact is that the richest countries in the world (in Europe and North America) have Christianity at their roots and continue to have Christianity as their main religion. So, however, do some of the poorer countries in the world (in Latin America) and it was in these countries that *liberation theology* was born in the 1970s. The author of the first book of theology I ever read, Leonardo Boff, was a Brazilian liberation theologian. The book's cover was bright red and had black prison bars bursting open in the middle. Being the first theology I encountered, liberation theology has never been for me a corrective to traditional theology; it has simply been *normal* theology, Christian theology. To this day, I am taken aback when reading theological treatises in which the issue of social justice is never addressed. " 'For I was hungry and you gave me no food, I was thirsty and you gave me nothing to drink, I was a stranger and you did not welcome me, naked and you did not give me clothing, sick and in prison and you did not visit me.' Then they also will answer, 'Lord, when was it that we saw you hungry or thirsty or a stranger or naked or sick or in prison, and did not take care of you?' Then he will answer them, 'Truly I tell you, just as you did not do it to one of the least of these, you did not do it to me'" (Matthew 25:35–40). It is God who talks in this passage in order to identify Herself quite clearly and directly with those who suffer for lack of material well-being.

In the fall of 2009 I visited Guatemala. In Uspantán, the village where the Maya leader and Nobel Prize winner Rigoberta Menchu was born, a small boy of five or six polished my shoes for a few coins before I climbed aboard a nine-seater jeep loaded with people; between those seated inside and those seated on the roof there were close to twenty of us. The jeep drove for a few hours on a dangerous winding road up to the tiny village of Lancetillo, in the middle of the jungle. Several times along the way we had to get off the jeep and help push it around a difficult turn or up a slope. It was in this area that tens of thousands of peasants from local "comunidades eclesiales de base" (ecclesial base communities) had organized themselves in the 1980s against the military dictatorships of Ríos Montt and Oscar Humberto Mejía Víctores. Thousands were horribly murdered by the military in one of the biggest massacres of the twentieth century. These peasants were convinced that their faith required them to oppose injustice and to help those in need. In Guatemala at that time, this meant risking one's life. I was deeply affected when I realized that all of this had been happening while I was in my early twenties: I was already Christian then and considered myself a socially conscious person – how did I not know about this massacre? I was going to mass every Sunday; why didn't we talk about what was happening in Guatemala?

In the context of the present economic crisis and the ongoing dismantling of the welfare state, many in Spain wish we could go back to "the good eighties." Whenever I hear this, I remember Guatemala. The 1980s meant massacre for Guatemala. Who was it that wanted to exploit the traditional land of the Maya peasants at the cost of tens of thousands of lives? And why? Rosa Luxemburg was convinced that capitalism, due to its constant need to expand, exports exploitation and destruction. Capitalism kills, often savagely, not by accident but out of structural need: it is based on competition and has to exploit in order to survive. In the 1980s, it was Latin America's turn. Now the exploitation and destruction has moved, at least partially, somewhere else, and it is taking its toll in Europe. Going back to the relative welfare of the 1980s is no solution. That would simply mean we have succeeded in pushing the crisis elsewhere. Going back is no solution: we need to move forward, beyond capitalism.

My opposition to capitalism has nothing to do with being against entrepreneurial initiative or private property. By my religious vows, I have renounced the right to hold individual private property and I consider this an advantage. But it is precisely because I appreciate the goodness of renouncing individual private property that I will never give support to a political regime that would *force* its citizens to give it up. Giving up individual private property in order to build a cooperative, for instance, can only work when the individuals involved are existentially motivated to do so. That being said, it is one thing to be against seizing all or most private property (and I am against it) and another to be ready to expropriate the excessive riches of a few to help the many in need, or to balance society and avoid abuse. I am in favor of expropriating the super-rich in order to help the poor, and in this I am in agreement with the social doctrine of the Roman Catholic Church when it clearly states that private property cannot be considered an *absolute* right. Nobody has the right to accumulate property unlimitedly while others starve as a consequence. Taking this seriously, as the present Pope Francis seems willing to do, would imply de facto declaring capitalism morally abhorrent and moving on with all urgency to start dismantling it – dismantling an economic system that produces enough food for 11 billion people on a planet of 7 billion while allowing close to 1 billion to suffer from chronic hunger; dismantling an economic system so intimately tied to the military industry that in order to survive it has to continually ignite wars that kill hundreds of thousands.

My critique of capitalism addresses the following three points: the capitalist notion of freedom; its orientation of economic activity to the maximization of profit; and its exploitation of workers.

The capitalist notion of freedom is a fallacy. From the protectionist policies of early capitalism to today's rescuing of banks "too big to fail," it is clear that capitalists have always counted on the support of the State to back them up, enacting favorable regulations and removing unfavorable ones. In nineteenth-century capitalism, the State protected the big industrial owners while leaving the children of the workers to toil in factories up to twelve hours a day and imprisoning their parents if they dared to demonstrate or to strike. In today's financial capitalism, the State bails out the big banks and passes their debts on to the people – it rescues banks in need while allowing those same banks to evict from their homes people who are in need, children included. Capitalism calls itself liberal, but is not an economic system based on freedom; it is an economic system based on *privilege*, that is, on the freedom of a few backed up by the power of the State. Today, the prime example of this is the Transatlantic Trade and Investment Partnership (TTIP), the free trade agreement being negotiated between the United States and the

European Union. This treaty would grant big corporations the right to sue a government whenever it implements a law or a regulation that goes against their private interests. How is this possible? What does it mean for a government to be legally bound to take into account the private interests of big corporations? Practically, it means the end of democracy. Democracy has to do with equal rights. Capitalism has to do – has always had to do – with privilege. They are incompatible. The TTIP prescribes that whenever a big corporation sues a government, the case needs to be resolved by an ad hoc international arbitration committee constituted by a representative of the corporation, a representative of the government and a third person agreed to by both parties. This arrangement effectively bypasses the public system of justice and its democratic controls.

The second point of my critique is the orientation of economic activity to the maximization of profit. Taking this orientation seriously has led capitalists to develop and implement "planned obsolescence" and the calculation of "opportunity costs." Both are short-term strategies that cause major and direct damage to people and to the planet and end up costing much more money than they create; in this sense, they are total economic failures. Why then are they implemented? The reason is simple and sad: the price of planned obsolescence and opportunity costs is not paid by the capitalists benefitting from them, but by the people and their governments. Planned obsolescence entails designing and manufacturing products that are not the best possible, but rather will break or stop working at a more or less predetermined time calculated to allow the capitalist to gain an economic advantage from the situation. For example, electric light bulbs are built with their incandescent parts too close, so that they fuse after a few thousand hours of use instead of lasting for over a hundred years, like the famous bulb in Pennsylvania; printers have a built-in chip that programs them to stop printing after a given number of pages. In both cases, the shorter lifespan of the product forces the consumer to buy a new one, thereby enabling the capitalist to make more money. Millions of bulbs and printers (to name only two items with planned obsolescence) are unnecessarily thrown into the garbage each week in order to increase the profits of a few companies. Who pays for taking care of the garbage – millions of items per day? Not the owners of those companies. The people pay, governments pay, the planet pays. But the capitalist makes a profit.

Calculating the opportunity costs means, for a capitalist, identifying where in the world his economic activity will be most profitable and moving his business there. Following this logic, countries that have minimal protections for workers and the environment are rewarded with a flourishing of economic activity while those that have greater protections are penalized. When a big business leaves, whole communities can be deprived of their livelihood. The greater the economic power of a big corporation, the stronger its capacity to force whole communities into accepting abusive working conditions. The incompatibility between capitalism and democracy again shows itself.

The third point of my critique concerns the exploitation of workers. Marx's critique of surplus value has taken a new twist with finance capitalism. Undoubtedly twenty-first-century capitalists continue making a profit from other people's work: the differential between the amount workers are paid in the sweatshops of Bangladesh and the benefit the capitalist obtains from their work is today in the order of the thousands. This direct form of surplus or exploitation continues, and there is no doubt that it weighs as heavily as it did in the nineteenth century upon those who are subjected to it. But this is not today the main form of capitalist exploitation; it is, rather, debt. Debt understood as "a financial product" that can be sold, merged, and split again in milliseconds on the financial markets. In less than a second, the fate of whole communities can be decided, and the one responsible for making that decision is not a person but a computer. Before any person has had the chance to analyze the consequences of the automated calculation, a new operation has already been completed that brings about a new set of concrete consequences: in a few seconds, businesses (and sometimes entire economic sectors or regions) can prosper or fail for no substantial reason other than lack of speculative muscle in the market, or by pure chance. Today's capitalists can buy the debt generated by the student loan of a promising freshman at Harvard university and then bundle it with the debt of a few other students from equally acclaimed universities to make a sum big enough to interest the market (or its computers). The bundled debt may then be sold for less than its nominal value, passing on to someone else the risk of not being paid; the new owner sells it on again and passes the risk to somebody else. The selling and buying of such "financial products" goes on uninterruptedly and makes up the most prosperous and important sector of today's global economy, which has therefore been described by some as a "casino economy."

In June 2012 I was invited to give the opening lecture at one of the most important conventions of Catalan businesspeople: up to 400 entrepreneurs were gathered in the Pyrenees for their 23rd annual meeting. My talk was entitled "Capitalism and ethics" and it developed at greater length the three points I have summarized above. The talk had a considerable impact; so much so that three weeks later I was invited to present my critique of capitalism on one of the most popular Catalan public TV programs. The public interest was overwhelming and I started to feel the pressure to engage politically in order to change the system I was criticizing. Four months later I received a visit from two leaders of a small Catalan anti-capitalist party with no parliamentary representation who thought I could play a role in helping create a kind of Catalan Syriza, a political movement capable of challenging the power of Catalan conservatives and the dominant neoliberal politics. I was not interested in creating a new political party, but I was highly motivated to help build the momentum for a political project that would combine the impulse to challenge capitalism with the drive for independence that was growing in strength in Catalonia. This was the beginning of Procés Constituent (Constituent Process), a political movement that was publicly announced by the economist Arcadi Oliveres and myself in April 2013, on the same public TV program where I had given my critique of capitalism ten months earlier. We presented a manifesto, and within three months more than 40,000 people had signed up and organized in more than seventy local chapters. Building a political movement from scratch like this has allowed me to gain a certain first-hand knowledge of contemporary politics. The experience has changed some of my views on alienation and on political parties.

Before engaging in politics, I had a discussion with my bishop about the value of doing so. In the 1970s, he had been in contact with some of the political activists involved in the Spanish transition from dictatorship to democracy and had learned an important lesson: *it is useless to change structures without changing hearts*. While agreeing that all structures can be corrupted and that no structure guarantees freedom, my view was (and still is) that there is no better opportunity for a change of heart than that brought about by a change – a real change – of structure. I have not learned this from Marx, but from the monastic tradition. Life in a monastery has strict rules that can feel hard to follow at the beginning. To be more precise, they are usually not so hard to follow at the *very* beginning but only a few months later, when the excitement of their novelty starts to dwindle. This is what happened to me: I had no problem following the rules in my one-month probation period in the summer of 1996, nor in the first six months after my entry in September 1997; the difficulties began when the initial enthusiasm waned and some of the structural demands of monastic life, like the diminished contact with the outside world or having to start and finish prayer at prescribed times, began to weigh heavily on me. The monastic structure pushed and challenged me, but I had the support of a wise teacher of novices who had a free heart and enough intelligence to periodically remind me – as Benedict in his Rule prescribes should be done – that the door was open for me to leave at any time. I accepted living, at least temporarily, under certain external conditions that I didn't like, and those conditions effected certain changes in me for which I am very thankful, such as deepening my self-awareness or clarifying some mystifying elements of my private prayer.

Before my monastic experience, my intensive medical training in the United States (1992–5) had also convinced me that structures can change hearts, and not always for the good: being on call every third night for most of my three-year medical residency in Buffalo, New York, hardened my heart, and I found myself saying and doing things to patients that I had strongly criticized in others as betraying a lack of respect or sensitivity. In Buffalo, I realized that even the weather conditions can change one's self-consciousness: some of my basic attitudes towards life (for instance, the perceived need to be disciplined and able to plan ahead) were very different in the moderate climate of my native Barcelona than in the freezing winter of Buffalo. Outside conditions, no question about it, do have the power to change hearts.

The dialectical relationship between consciousness and external conditions seems today to have brought a majority of people in Western societies to the belief that there can be no alternative to capitalism. I have found that it is relatively easy to attract popular support when criticizing capitalism and pointing out its obvious deficiencies, particularly in today's Spain. It is an altogether different matter, however, to engage in concrete political action to bring about the desired change. An emotional motivation of great intensity seems necessary to break the inertia of the status quo and overcome the fear of change, and in Catalonia today – as in many places in the past – this emotional motivation is being supplied by nationalism. For some people, nationalism is inherently attached to chauvinism and xenophobia. I am among those who defend the positive potential of nationalism to make concrete in time and space (in a given history and a given land) a personal commitment that goes beyond one's own self, one's own family, and one's own ideological community. I believe Iceland would not have been able to resist the impositions of the Troika without a concrete sense of national pride, and the same can be said (despite the sad final outcome) for Greece.

Understandably, the left has tended to shun nationalism as bourgeois ideology. Nationalist wars led workers to kill one another defending the privileges of ruling elites; socialism was and is internationalist: *Workers of the world, unite*, see where your interests lie, realize who your allies are, and identify with the class struggle as an international struggle. Nevertheless, the left has not always rejected nationalism. The Irish socialist James Connolly, for instance, clearly distinguished the right to self-determination from bourgeois interests, as did Mahatma Gandhi. Venezuela's former president Hugo Chávez, like all proponents of Bolivarian socialism, explicitly appealed to the sense of national humiliation felt by Latin Americans vis-à-vis their historical colonization and their present dependency on the United States.

In October 2014, I was asked by the British newspaper the *Guardian* to publish an article on Catalan independence. Here is what I wrote:

WHY I WANT INDEPENDENCE FOR CATALONIA

I am Catalan and I have two reasons to want Catalonia to become an independent state as soon as possible. The first is to improve the quality of our democracy, and the second is to preserve and foster cultural diversity.

Having a smaller political unit allows greater democratic accountability. The determinants and consequences of political decisions can be better grasped at a smaller scale because the citizens have first-hand knowledge of the issues at stake: decisions that affect the landscape, conflicts among different social groups, the allocation of resources, alternative sources of energy, the potential for economic development of specific areas, the need to preserve natural beauties...

Having first-hand knowledge of these issues at the grassroots level does not exclude experts from being hired, when needed, to study certain problems and propose solutions, but it allows the people to have a much better critical appraisal of the experts' work and their proposals. The quality of this critical appraisal corresponds to the quality of a democracy.

Most citizens in a small country the size of Catalonia (32,000 sq km with 7.5 million inhabitants) not only have an objective knowledge of the issues at stake with regard to particular political decisions, but – most important – are subjectively involved in them. They care about them because these decisions will – one way or another – directly impact on their lives or on those of the people they love.

A smaller political unit allows for a more humane political experience. In a smaller country, social activists and people working at the grassroots level have a greater chance of knowing each other personally and being able to pass on to each other relevant information in a direct manner; they also have a greater chance of knowing most of their political representatives personally.

Besides the structural link between size and democracy, I see contingent reasons that make me expect that an independent Catalonia will enjoy a better democracy. The "indignados" movement in Spain, which started in 2011, has identified many deficiencies in the country's democracy: corruption is rampant and not being adequately investigated; the financing of the political parties is not transparent; there is no mechanism to depose political representatives who contradict their political program and rule against the will of the people who voted for them; people are evicted from their homes by the same banks that profited from the rescue money provided by the European Union (the banks are rescued, the people are not); the health system is being privatized against the will of the majority; rich people pay comparatively less tax than those who are poor; renewable energy is not being developed despite there being enough natural resources and a popular will to do so; and city halls are being stripped of their decision-making power.

Independence for Catalonia is no guarantee that these issues will be resolved, but having to write and approve a new constitution would be a unique opportunity to work towards solutions to these problems in a much more comprehensive and radical way than is possible in an already constituted state. Many in Catalonia expect that the process of drafting a new constitution will elicit a political debate from the bottom up that could radically rethink our economic system, so that in the new Catalonia people and their basic needs cannot be treated as commodities. Many also expect a radical rethinking of our political system, so that institutions empower the people instead of stifling them with bureaucracy.

Along with improving the quality of our democracy, my other motivation in wanting independence for Catalonia is the fostering of cultural diversity. I do not consider our language, traditions, and history better than anybody else's and I do not consider them in any way pure or able to be distinguished essentially from those of any other group of people. Our language and traditions are the result of complex processes of cultural cross-fertilisation and, as long as they are alive, I expect them to continue happily resisting rigid definition.

In their contingency and fluidity they contribute to the world's cultural diversity, and I expect the government of an independent Catalonia to celebrate and foster them in a much more congenial way than the Spanish central government currently does. (*Guardian*, November 3, 2014)

3   Sext: public health

The morning is over and with it more than half of our working hours. The motto *ora et labora* (pray and work), despite not being found in the Benedictine Rule, captures well our monastic routine: five daily hours of prayer and six of work. Just over two and a half hours of prayer take place in the morning: matins, personal prayer, and lauds are half an hour each, the Eucharist around forty-five minutes, and the midday prayer (called sext because it takes place six hours after sunrise) around twenty. The rest are in the evening: vespers are half an hour, then follows an hour and a half of personal prayer called "lectio," and the day ends with twenty minutes of compline. Four of the daily working hours are in the morning, between breakfast and sext, and two are in the afternoon, between lunch and vespers.

The prayer of sext comes right before lunch. Cortisol levels are already declining and the level of body energy is not comparable to that in the early morning. It is often the moment of realizing that the work planned in the morning will probably not be accomplished by the end of the day. It is the peak of the heat in summer, and the time of the "meridian demon" of the monastic tradition, also known as "acedia": a feeling of disgust with one's life or even with life in general; a feeling of meaninglessness, of futility, a lack of energy and existential motivation. According to the monastic tradition, the problem is not having such feelings (occasional acedia is to be expected when self-awareness is high); the problem is yielding to them.

Midday reminds us that we are not only spirit; we are also body, and the body needs to be taken into account. We need nourishment and rest. The liturgy of the hours adapts itself to the rhythm of nature and human physiology and helps to harmonize the mind and the body: the nocturnal prayer of matins is meditative and deep, the lauds at sunrise are joyful and full of promise, the midday prayer accompanies failing strength and the need for rest, the vespers at dusk are the moment of faith, and the compline before going to bed the moment of forgiveness. Body and mind are thankful for a routine respectful of their natural rhythms, but modern medicine has moved far away from this ancient wisdom.

A few months after I entered the monastery, sister M. Tecla, an old sister with no college education, showed me her collection of medicinal plants: field horsetail for the kidneys, chamomile for digestion, lemon verbena for the lungs, elderberry for the flu, thyme for cough, Valerian root, St. John's wort, and a few others. Sister M. Tecla collected the plants herself, dried them, and prepared the infusions for the sick sisters; having learnt that I was a medical doctor, she wanted to discuss with me some of her plants' properties. She looked at me in disbelief when I told her that I had no idea, absolutely none, about the medical properties of any plants. Over the years, I have picked up some of her wisdom on the matter and now use and prescribe some herbs for certain ailments.

Bad as it is, the main problem of modern medicine is not its move away from a certain ancient wisdom. The main problem is its commodification under capitalist market conditions: turning the care of the sick and the prevention of disease into stock market transactions; allowing huge profits and financial operations to depend on the selling of medical products, the delivery of medical treatment or, more particularly, the medical insuring of the healthy or the chronically ill. In the 1980s, in an attempt to bring her country up to the standards of the US, the British Prime Minister Margaret Thatcher started dismantling the excellent National Health Service. Other European countries have since followed suit. In the year 2000, the World Health Organization (WHO) published a list of the 191 countries that then belonged to the WHO ranked by the quality of their medical systems. The assessment was made according to very basic criteria: life expectancy, healthy life expectancy, and infant mortality, and it also took into account the cost per capita measured in international dollars. France and Italy ranked first and second respectively while the United Kingdom was eighteenth and the United States thirty-seventh;

Spain was number seven. Other rankings produced in 2010 and 2013, using data from the Organisation for Economic Cooperation and Development, were also consistent in showing that countries with universal public health systems have the best outcomes and spend the least money per capita. Despite this overwhelming data, there is today in Spain, and particularly in Catalonia, a very aggressive attempt by the conservative ruling parties in central and local governments to privatize the public health system: hospitals are being sold to high-risk capital corporations and private companies are being contracted to provide services previously carried out by civil servants. We are taking now the same path that the United Kingdom took in the 1980s, without acknowledging its deleterious effects or the fact that, in the following decade, Tony Blair's government had to recognize the urgent need to put a brake on Thatcher's privatizing policies in the domain of public health.

Privatization today affects not only city hospitals and national public health systems but also the biggest health authority worldwide, the WHO. Since the late 1990s, the WHO's financing has come to depend more on extraordinary donations from private foundations (the most important of them being the Bill & Melinda Gates Foundation) than on the ordinary contributions of its member states. This situation severely compromises the independence of the WHO and its capacity to confront big economic powers in order to defend public health. In March 2014, I delivered a lecture at the Johns Hopkins Bloomberg School of Public Health, presenting evidence that during the 2009 flu pandemic, the WHO largely ignored the interests of the public in favor of those of the major pharmaceutical corporations. The lecture was later published in the *International Journal of Health Services* with the title "Flu Vaccination: the gap between evidence and public policy." Here are some of my final remarks:

> *The research presented in this article exposes a wide gap between evidence and public policy with regard to influenza vaccination in the context of the 2009 pandemic and yearly seasonal epidemics. This is both hard to accept and difficult to ignore. It is hard to accept because it shows that the WHO and health authorities*

worldwide failed to protect the interests of the most vulnerable during the 2009 flu pandemic, fostering instead the interests of a few big corporations. It is also hard to accept because it calls into question seasonal flu vaccination campaigns, a well-established practice recommended for decades by the WHO and by most public health authorities worldwide. At the same time, the data presented are difficult to ignore because the lack of a scientific basis for seasonal flu vaccination campaigns has been repeatedly attested since 2006 by epidemiologists from top-tier institutions, including Tom Jefferson from the Cochrane Collaboration, Lisa Jackson from the Group Health Center for Health Studies in Seattle, and Lone Simonsen from the School of Public Health at George Washington University, to name a few. Why have their recommendations not been heard? Why do health authorities at local, national, and international levels ignore their solid, evidence-based expert advice? Margaret McCartney, elected in 2013 to the Royal College of General Practitioners (United Kingdom), in a brief and pointed contribution to the British Medical Journal *at the start of the 2014 influenza season, raised the question of what use is mass flu vaccination and concluded that, "in view of the available evidence, the current policy is impossible to justify."* (*International Journal of Health Services*, 45:3, 2015, pp. 453–70)

The health committee of the British House of Commons had already reported in 2005 that the pharmaceutical industry was having an undue influence on health policy and health education in the UK, and issued a list of ninety-four urgent recommendations, among them the proposal that the public health system be given the capacity to carry out its own studies of drug efficacy and safety, independently of the interests of the companies that sell the drugs. This recommendation has thus far failed to lead to any new laws or regulations. Currently, in the UK as in the rest of Europe, studies on the efficacy and safety of drugs remain in the hands of pharmaceutical companies that have been accused on numerous occasions of betraying the trust placed in them; moreover, the office that grants licenses to commercialize drugs – the European Medicines Agency (EMA) – receives over 50 percent of its funding from these same companies.

In 2014, after a coordinated and sustained effort from some of the most conscientious members of the medical scientific community, the EMA agreed to force pharmaceutical companies to allow medical scientists to have full access to all relevant data on medications commercialized in Europe. This regulation has not yet been fully implemented. The situation today is such that a medical researcher has no full and unrestricted access to the scientific information that would allow her to critically assess industry recommendations with regard to the indications, dosage, or side-effects of any given medication. Although the EMA agreed to grant such access in 2014, they postponed the full implementation of the regulation until 2016, after coming under pressure from the big pharmaceutical corporations. It is important to note that in 2016 the big corporations – pharmaceutical and otherwise – expect to have the TTIP (the free trade agreement between the EU and the US) approved; if this proves to be the case, the hard-won right to gain access to medical research information might be outlawed again to protect the interests of the industry over patients' interests. It is also important to note that in 2007 the pharmaceutical company Merck – which manufactures Gardasil, the controversial vaccine against the human papilloma virus – pleaded guilty in a US criminal court to having hidden vital information regarding the safety of its anti-inflammatory blockbuster drug Vioxx (rofecoxib). First approved in 1999, Vioxx may have caused the death by heart attack or stroke of more than 27,000 people before it was taken off the market in 2004. Merck was ordered by the court to pay millions of dollars, but despite being extremely high, the fine was less than the total profit Merck had made from selling the drug. None of the businessmen responsible for this crime went to jail, and the company has been allowed to continue doing business as usual.

Allowing big corporations to seek to maximize their profits in selling health products and services has led to the "medicalization" of life and society. The concept of medicalization is not new, but it has changed its meaning in the last few decades, coinciding with the growth in the health industry's power. In the nineteenth century and until the 1960s, the word "medicalization" was used to describe the process by which a society adopted public health measures that resulted in a decrease in illness, disability, and death in the population: ensuring sewage collection and disposal, water sanitation, access to drinkable water and safe and decent housing, outlawing childhood labor, regulating slaughter-houses, and draining marshes to avoid mosquito-borne illnesses, etc. In each of these cases, medical experts were consulted and the implementation of their recommendations led to a clear and immediate reduction in the burden of illness and the need for medical intervention. Not so today. In today's medicalized societies, consult-ing medical experts and implementing the changes in public policy that they recommend actually *increases* rather than reduces the burden of illness and the need for medical intervention. This is a fundamental difference having to do with the interests of private companies that profit from selling medical products and services. Med-icalization today increases the burden of disease and the need for medical intervention because it expands the category of disease to include con-ditions that were not considered pathological a few decades ago; for instance, hair loss in men, mood swings in teenagers, or menopause. In some individual cases, such conditions may indeed need medical treatment; however, contemporary medicalization implies that *all cases* require intervention and approves public health campaigns to convince the population that what they used to consider a "normal" condition (hair loss in men, etc.) is in fact "pathological."

There is no question that today we live longer than our grandparents' generation did, take many more medicines and visit many more doctors. This might lead one to conclude that contemporary medicalization is working after all, but this is not the case. The most important determinant of health and life expectancy is not lack of medical care; it is poverty. People who eat, drink, and sleep enough, have decent housing, and are not overworked live longer regardless of their degree of medicalization. This is why life expectancy in Japan is consistently higher than in the UK or the US, despite the latter countries being much more medicalized than Japan. In 2013, the WHO reported that Japan had the longest life expectancy of all: 84 years (80 for men and 87 for women); the UK was nineteenth with 81 years (79 for men and 83 for women) and the US thirty-fourth with 79 years (76 for men and 81 for women). The US is by far the most medicalized society, but it is a long way from being the healthiest.

Solid and striking evidence of the link between social vulnerability and mortality in contemporary European societies has been provided recently by researchers David Stuckler, Professor of Political Economy and Sociology at Oxford, and Sanjay Basu, Assistant Professor of Medicine at Stanford. In 2013 they published a book entitled *The Body Economic: Why Austerity Kills*, demonstrating that the cuts in social programs imposed on Greece and Spain by the Troika (the European Commission, the European Central Bank, and the International Monetary Fund) caused an increase in the overall mortality in those countries during the crisis. In Iceland, by contrast, the rejection of austerity measures and the decision to increase spending on social programs from 21 percent to 25 percent of GDP between 2007 and 2009 led to an improvement of health indexes without an increase in medical expenditure.

Allocating more and more financial and human resources to meet the demands of an expanding private medical industry is clearly not the way to address public health policy today. There is an urgent need to separate the medical needs of the population from the private interests of big corporations. This is the argument of a recent book by the Danish epidemiologist Peter Gøtzche, *Deadly Medicines and Organized Crime: How Big Pharma Has Corrupted Healthcare*, which won the 2014 British Medical Association book prize in the Basis of Medicine category. Gøtzche illustrates his argument with multiple examples. In some of them, like the Vioxx case mentioned earlier, big pharmaceutical companies have acted criminally, withheld information, published misleading reports about the efficacy or the safety of their drugs, and caused avoidable death or disability as a consequence. In other cases, they have acted according to the law but their actions have had devastating effects because public health policies are increasingly drafted to suit their interests rather than help patients. For example, it is not against the law to commercialize a drug produced by introducing a minor change in the chemical structure of the active molecule of an already existing drug without altering its efficacy. Drugs obtained by this process are called "me-too drugs" or "follow-on drugs." These types of drugs represent today *the vast majority* of the new drugs being developed by the pharmaceutical industry. It seems absurd: why would any company invest time and money developing a new drug that has no substantial difference from an old one, a new drug that is not really *new* at all? The answer is that me-too drugs, despite not representing any real innovation, can be patented as "new," and whenever a pharmaceutical company is granted a new patent it automatically acquires the right to commercialize it for the next twenty years as a monopoly. This means there is a big incentive for companies to produce me-too drugs in order to replace older drugs that are about to lose their patent, because losing the monopoly means competing with companies that will produce generic versions of the drug and sell it for a much lower price. In such conditions, there is really no incentive for the industry to risk losing money by researching truly pioneer drugs, the only ones that could bring hope to people suffering from illnesses that today are still incurable. Instead, pharmaceutical companies concentrate their efforts on producing yet another painkiller, statin, or anti-acid.

The millions of dollars spent by pharmaceutical companies on their drugs are not for research and development but for marketing. Having a patent for a me-too drug is only profitable if patients/physicians choose to buy/prescribe it instead of buying/prescribing the older drug in generic form. This is why the main activity of the big pharmaceuticals today is advertising and lobbying instead of researching. Public universities, big public hospitals, and not-for-profit health organizations are still able to pursue innovative science, but they lack the capacity to develop commercial products derived from their research and discoveries. Consequently, public health institutions are forced to sell their findings to private industry, and these findings are then submitted to the rule of profit maximization. Regardless of their potential for alleviating suffering and illness, some of these innovative discoveries are only used today to obtain so-called "defensive patents": a company will buy them not in order to develop a medication or health product but simply to block a competitor from doing so. Whether a new drug is developed at all or is stopped in its tracks by a "defensive patent" depends not on its therapeutic potential but on whether a private company can make profit from it or not.

The existence of me-too drugs is one of the reasons why Peter Gøtzche's claim that big pharma *corrupts* healthcare is a sad and literal description. The *Oxford English Dictionary* defines "corruption" as the "destruction or dissolution of the constitution which makes a thing what it is." Healthcare is made what it is by its capacity to take care of the medical needs of the population. To orient healthcare towards increasing the private profits of a few corporations is to corrupt it. But the problem is not philosophical, concerning the theoretical loss of the healthcare system's essence; it is rather the concrete consequences that derive from this: besides blocking innovation and holding promising discoveries hostage, the release of me-too drugs into the market has the potential to cause hitherto unknown side-effects that may be damaging and even lethal. Even if a drug's main function is preserved, introducing a change, however minor, into its molecular structure can trigger unexpected side-effects that might not have been identified in the clinical trials leading to its approval. Discovering serious unexpected side-effects is always a potential problem when releasing a new drug. Only after millions of people have been exposed to it can the safety profile of a drug be established with some certainty. Since this risk is unavoidable it is acceptable when releasing drugs that are real innovations, but it is totally unacceptable when releasing drugs whose only purpose is to increase the monopoly profits of private companies. Producing me-too drugs is the pharmaceutical industry's responsibility, but granting patents for them and licensing them for medical use is that of health authorities. Private companies cannot corrupt the health system by themselves; the collusion of governments is necessary. Instead of complaining about the rapacious nature of private companies, let us organize politically so that limits can be set on them. It is both our right and our responsibility.

The midday prayer of "sext" is over. Now it is time for lunch.

4 Recreation: feminism

An hour before sunset the bell rings again. This time it doesn't call us to prayer but to *recreation*, the daily gathering of the community to share worries and joys and to interact with each other at a personal level. Recreation is different from the gathering that we call *chapter* and also from the one we call *assembly*. The chapter meeting takes place once a week and is so called because it consists of reading a chapter from the Rule of Benedict and then commenting on it. Traditionally, the abbess would be the only one giving the commentary and then applying it to the present life of the community. Nowadays it is also common – and this is the case in our monastery

– for those sisters who wish to do so to share their own thoughts after the abbess' comments. The atmosphere of the chapter meeting is meditative. It is considered a spiritual practice, conducive to deepening one's consciousness and practical understanding of the monastic life. The monastic *assembly*, on the other hand, does not have a fixed periodicity, but is called by the abbess whenever there is a need to make an important decision.

The daily recreation, unlike chapter and assembly, has a much lighter tone; nevertheless, since my first weeks at the monastery it has seemed to me the most important time of the day because it is the most unregulated. The atmosphere of recreation gives the precise measure of the vitality of the community. Sometimes it is tense, quarrelsome, uncomfortable; at other times boring, repetitive, or superficial. There needs to be at least one sister ready to break with convention and be herself for recreation to have meaning; when several do so, the recreation becomes lively, authentic, unexpected, complex. Such real exchanges break down my barriers and narrow securities and open me up to start understanding something about who

God is or what She wants: "I give you a new commandment: love each other, as I have loved you" (John 13:34). "A new commandment" is my maxim, the words inscribed on the ring I was given on the day of my solemn vows (in April 2003). It is a quotation from the Gospel of John by which Jesus expresses the need to move beyond the Law: it is necessary to have laws and to value the Law, but it is vital to understand that Love is above the Law. What this means concretely in everyday life is for each person to ascertain.

Upon entering the monastery, I was deeply touched by the way in which the abbess conducted herself at recreation. She was surprisingly quick and gracious in disarming aggression or potential conflicts. During one of my first recreations, a resentful sister launched into a critique without specifying against whom she was speaking and at once a tension could be felt in the group. The abbess was not the intended target of the criticism and she knew it, but the critique was so vague that anyone could have felt it was directed at them. The abbess took it upon herself in a simple manner, with no sarcasm or reproach, and the tension vanished as quickly as it had appeared. After that, the criticizing sister looked thankful and spoke with a different expression and tone of voice. I thought I had witnessed a miracle. The abbess consistently acted in this way and I came to appreciate that many other sisters, particularly the older ones, did likewise: not turning away to avoid problems, but making sure pettiness never gained the upper hand.

As a child, I was raised with a sense of entitlement to all that life had to offer with no discrimination whatsoever because of my sex. This was how my parents raised both of my sisters and me. But I had an uncle, whom I admired, who used to challenge me: "You're only a girl!"; and I was surrounded by a patriarchal culture that I was deeply internalizing without noticing it. A mathematics teacher in primary school, whom I particularly loved, used to say about women: "Long hair, short ideas!" I cut my hair short and wanted to be a boy. I masculinized my name and got used to having boys rather than girls as my main playmates and friends. After menstruation began, I separated from the boys and started to have girls as best friends, but a sense of inadequacy remained, a sense of disadvantage in being a girl, in being a woman.

I encountered feminism in my twenties and started to become conscious of my problematic feminine identity, but it was not until entering the monastery and sharing my daily life with forty women that I realized to what extent I still believed that being a woman was a fate to be regretted. It must have been two or three years after my entrance that the abbess told me how she had also struggled with the fact of being a woman in a world that associated womanhood with restricted personal freedom and personal options, and how one day, around the age of fifty, she had awakened to the inner joy of her femininity. She didn't try to explain what "her femininity" was, but the matter-of-fact way in which she talked about it shook me. While my head was busy deconstructing the notion of "femininity," my entrails were yearning.

I learned feminist theology with the biblical scholar Elisabeth Schüssler Fiorenza. I was her translator at a conference in Barcelona in 1992, translated her book on biblical hermeneutics *But She Said* in 1993–4, and, thanks to her letter of recommendation, studied from 1995–7, just before entering the monastery, at the Harvard Divinity School where she was a professor. At the time, I was convinced that "femininity" and "masculinity" were simply cultural categories. Today I believe that they are indeed cultural, *but not only*. I believe that what we call sexual or gender *culture* gives a name to – and tries to shape and fix according to certain presuppositions, fears, or interests – something that exists regardless of culture, namely, that the majority of newborns have either a vagina or a penis and that the majority of adults of fertile age can either impregnate or become pregnant. However, these basic biological differences are by no means universal. There are many people who don't conform to this simple binary distribution, and their existence needs to be taken into account in order to speak properly of human sexuality, without forcing it into falsely universal categories and considering all deviations from the binary norm to be pathological. The differences are not universal, but they are dominant: the majority of newborns and the majority of adults manifest them. This dominant but nevertheless non-universal sexual dimorphism (penis vs. vagina, ability to impregnate vs. ability to get pregnant) is reinforced in its dual character by the infantile need to define oneself with regard to one's mother. I agree with the psychoanalytic notion that the psyche of a child is wholeheartedly oriented towards the mother as its first object of desire. I believe that in early childhood (up to six years of age) the mother occupies almost the totality, and certainly the most important part, of the desiring horizon of the child. As the consciousness of self develops, the child is forced to compare its body with that of its reference figure, the mother: is my body like hers? Is it different?

During my doctoral work in medicine, after celebrating my first monastic profession (temporal vows) in the year 2000, I had the opportunity to experience the strength of the newborn's attachment when I conducted research with premature babies exposed to the recorded voice of their mother. For ten days during the novitiate, I had listened for three hours a day to Gregorian chant, Mozart, and the recorded voice of my mother filtered above 8,000 hertz, as part of a technique called the *Tomatis method*. This method is used to improve one's ability to sing, but its most interesting effects are psychological. I was curious about the technique and travelled to Carcassonne to visit Dr. Tomatis, the French ear, nose, and throat specialist after whom the

method is named, and then to Lyon to visit one
of his closest collaborators, Dr. Petijean. Dr.
Petijean had demonstrated in his doctoral dissertation that the voice of the pregnant mother
reaches the fetus travelling not externally through
the air and across her abdomen but internally
through her spine. Because of the impedance of
the bone, the harmonics of the mother's voice
most easily transmitted are those above 8,000
hertz. These harmonics create a vibration within
the uterus that the outer membrane of the developing embryo, the skin of the fetus and finally
also the developing fetal ears and brain are able
to perceive. This vibration has the unique char-
acteristic of corresponding with the hormones
circulating within the embryonic and fetal cells
because they are the hormones of the mother
and vary, like her voice, according to her emo-
tions. If the mother is upset, her body secretes
adrenaline and her voice becomes louder or
tenser; the embryo and the fetus perceive the
change in vibration that corresponds to the
mother's voice together with the effects of
the adrenaline in their tissues. If the mother is
experiencing pleasure, her voice modulates
accordingly and her body secretes endorphins;

the embryo and the fetus perceive the change in modulation together with the new hormonal input and start connecting the reactions of their innermost cells and tissues with a particular stimulus that comes from the outside (the vibrations above 8,000 hertz). Experiments with newborn babies demonstrate not only that they are able to recognize the voice of their mother without ever having heard it extra-uterus, but also, most importantly, that they exhibit such a drive towards it that the mother's voice can be used to condition their behavior: newborn babies that are rewarded by hearing the voice of their mother only when sucking in a pattern predetermined by the researchers, learn to do so in a few hours; the babies are able to change their natural way of sucking in order to obtain the reward of listening to the recorded voice of their mother.

The depth of the existential link to one's mother cannot be overemphasized: it lies at the bottom of our psychic structure and holds it together; it is constitutive of our identity as individuals. Only by deepening our understanding of the mother–child relationship will we be able to start ascertaining what is at stake when we discuss sexual identity or gender, masculinity, and femininity. Many are doing so, but their voice and their studies are stifled amidst dominant discourses that over-determine sexuality either from a biological or from a cultural perspective. The psychoanalyst Julia Kristeva has taken into account the depth of the bond between mother and child in her analysis of the violence that some men exert over the women who are their sexual or sentimental partners. Kristeva points to the fact that we have all, whether women or men, had the body and the psyche of a woman at our disposal when we were babies; the body and psyche of a woman ready at almost all times to satisfy our emotional and physical needs; a feminine body, a warm bosom and two welcoming breasts at our disposal to nourish us, shelter us, and protect us. One of the most ancient names the Bible gives to God is *El-Shaddai*; some scholars believe that it should be translated as "God with two Breasts," but it is usually translated as "God the Almighty" (as in Psalm 91). Our first experience of benevolent power is directly linked to the breasts of the mother that give us life and without which we would die. This helps us to understand why, when they are existentially challenged, immature men feel entitled to receive physical and emotional satisfaction from the women they love, while immature women feel guilty for not providing unconditional physical and emotional satisfaction to the men they love. The deeper the immaturity, the greater the possibility that the entitlement felt by immature men will turn into physical violence, and the culpability felt by immature women into submission.

Full maturity can never be taken for granted. Even without falling into violent relationships, men might confuse personal freedom with fear of dependency (the fear of relying too much on those one loves to the point of being unable to conceive of one's life without them), and women might confuse love with fear of solitude (the fear of conceiving of oneself as truly separated and distinct from those one loves).

Despite many advances towards equality, in today's world millions of girls are not able to attend school as their brothers do and are not able to choose their husband or whether they even want one; millions of women are not able to terminate their marriage if they are unhappy or even when they are abused, are not able to own property or allowed to earn their own living. A report presented in Brussels in July 2015 by the European Parliament's Committee on Civil Liberties, Justice and Home Affairs showed that the majority of girls travelling alone in search of asylum in the EU don't reach their destination, while the majority of boys do; the girls fall prey to human-trafficking networks operating in Europe while EU governments turn their heads away. According to a 2006 US Department of State report on human trafficking, 800,000 women are trafficked across borders and forced into prostitution every year; half of them are under-age. According to a 2009 report from the United Nations, 270,000 of these women are trafficked within the EU. In 2012, the *New York Times* revealed that Goldman Sachs had a 16 percent share in the biggest forum for sex trafficking of under-age girls in the United States: a website called backpage.com. In 2014, former US president Jimmy Carter urged governments to adopt the Nordic model to fight prostitution, decriminalizing the women and criminalizing their clients and all third parties involved.

On a less dramatic note, in the year 2000 the women of the city of Barcelona worked on average twice as many hours as the men and received half their salary. In addition to holding down a full-time job, the majority of women dedicated fifteen hours or more per week to domestic chores while the majority of men dedicated seven hours or less per week to them. Leaving aside domestic work, in Europe the salary a woman receives for a paid job is on average still 16 percent lower than that of a man performing at the same level and with similar qualifications.

Despite these obvious inequalities, feminist consciousness and identification has been rather in decline among women over the last twenty years. Today, most men and women in Western countries adamantly refuse gender discrimination and injustice and are ready to challenge it in the concrete cases that confront them personally, but they don't feel drawn to a systemic analysis of the wider problem and tend to disregard the work and the accumulated wisdom of the feminist movement. There is a renewed interest in the gender difference that increasingly seems to lead female teenagers into accepting controlling behaviors from their male partners that their mothers would have flatly refused (for instance, agreeing not to go out whenever their male partner is away or busy, or allowing him to check their cell phone messages and calls). At the same time, girls and female teenagers are subject to the strong pressure of a cultural hyper-sexualization that impels them to try to make their bodies conform to absurd standards of beauty that are impossible to achieve. One of my teenage nieces recently informed me about the "thigh-gap" vogue: young women are led to believe that having beautiful thighs requires there to be a space between them when standing upright with the knees together. Anatomically, this ideal of beauty can only be achieved by girls with an androgynous pelvis or by girls with a non-androgynous pelvis who have emaciated thighs. A few years ago, I became aware of a growing tendency in genital cosmetic surgery: an increasing number of teenagers and adult women believe that, in order to be beautiful, their labia minora must be shorter than their labia majora, and so need to be cut if they are longer; cutting the labia minora eliminates a very sensitive tissue capable of swelling when aroused, substituting it with an insensitive scar that sometimes proves painful. The thigh-gap and the short labia minora can easily be faked using computer programs that digitally modify images, and such programs are indeed regularly used by the editors of magazines that portray naked women. The proliferation of digitally altered images of women seems to be at the origin of the current rise of such unreasonable expectations of female beauty.

Being a Roman Catholic nun, I am often questioned about my feminism, as if being a nun and being a feminist were incompatible and one of the two has to be inauthentic. I became a feminist before I became a nun, but I became a feminist thanks to the study of theology, of feminist liberation theology. I learned that man and woman were created equally in the image of God and that in the Letter to the Galatians Saint Paul made clear that in Christ Jesus, in the new life of the Christian, the differences between male and female do not count: all human beings are created equal in the image of God and are equally called to full maturity by becoming like Christ. The patristic theology we read every morning at matins clearly states that "God became human so that the human can become God," and doesn't shrink from using the word *theosis*, that is, divinization, when describing the goal and purpose of human life: *theosis*, divinization, full participation in God's freedom and love, friendship with God, communion. The notion of "being as communion" derives from the notion of God as community (God as Trinity) and presupposes the inseparability of freedom and love. Patriarchal culture, on the contrary, presupposes that women are by nature more loving than free while men are by nature more free than loving, and points to the heterosexual union of the two as the condition of a fulfilled personal life. As long as the mother-figure remains the hidden reference of human desire, I believe that patriarchal stereotypes are unavoidable: women will tend to fear solitude and men will tend to fear dependency. However, the mother-figure does not need to remain the reference of human desire. "How can a man be born when he is old? Can he enter a second time into his mother's womb, and be born?" Such is the amazed reaction of Nicodemus, a scholar in first-century Palestine, to Jesus of Nazareth, when Jesus links the fact of "seeing the kingdom of God" – that is, achieving personal fulfillment, becoming a realized human being – to the fact of "being born again." "Verily, verily, I say unto you, except a man be born of water and of the Spirit, he cannot enter into the kingdom of God. That which is born of the flesh is flesh; and that which is born of the Spirit is spirit. Marvel not that I said unto you, you must be born again. The wind blows where it wills, and you hear the sound thereof, but cannot tell whence it comes, and whither it goes: so is every one that is born of the Spirit" (John 3:3–8). The distinction between "flesh" and "Spirit" – that which is born of the flesh is flesh; and that which is born of the Spirit is spirit – has here nothing to do with a denigration of the body, but concerns the lack of freedom, the inertia that ensues when the Spirit is dormant and the body becomes dominated by automatism or routine; hence the need to be born again in an unexpected and original way. Being adult, fulfilled, divinized, fully human means being able to abandon the childhood reference (the mother) and to take instead not the Father with a capital "F" but "the water and the Spirit." This is what I consider the foundation of queer theology: our human fulfillment is not subject to categories of any kind; it comes about only when one is ready to acknowledge one's own uniqueness, one's own originality. People who have sexual identities that do not fit the socially predominant categories embody a queerness that in the deepest sense applies to us all because of our having been created in the image of God and called to be like God. The fifth-century Christian theologian Augustine of Hippo wrote: "O, man, you were created without you, you will not be saved without you." You were born "of the flesh" without you (were born in a way that lacked freedom; you had no choice in it); you will not be saved (born again) without you (being born again can only be free; it won't happen if you don't want it). To be created "in the image of God" means to be able to be free and loving.

The challenge of "queerness," of personal uniqueness, of freedom has been a cause of constant struggle among those who have called themselves Christians. I have already highlighted in the first chapter some very early Christian texts (belonging to the New Testament) that call us to radical freedom and that were preserved together with other equally old texts that uphold authoritarian social institutions. The call to freedom (coming from God) and the fear of freedom (coming from human mistrust) were both present at the beginning of Christianity and continue to be present today: some statements, some practices, some institutional routines of the Church have nothing to do with fostering full personal freedom and responsibility. The Roman Catholic Church, my Church, is structurally sexist: it discriminates against women in the sense that it preserves all key institutional positions for those who have received priestly ordination and at the same time precludes women from receiving such an ordination. Many women of the Church are working to change this situation and I am among them, but I know many others who either don't think the issue is a priority or don't think that people (whether men or women) should be ordained at all. I agree with the need to critique all forms of clerical power, but I distinguish this critique from the scandal of discrimination: whatever form priestly ordination might take, it is discriminatory to exclude women from it.

In 2007, I published *Feminist Theology in History*, a book that cost me tears but also brought me great joys. I studied fourteen women from the fourteenth century to the eighteenth who were encouraged and inspired by their Christian faith to overcome the discrimination against women in their time and to challenge the theology that gave support to such discrimination. These women were: Christine de Pizan, Moderata Fonte, Lucrezia Marinella, Isabel de Villena, Teresa of Ávila, Juana Inés de la Cruz, María Jesús de Ágreda, Bathsua Makin, Marie de Gournay, Anna Maria van Schurman, Mary Astell, Elena Cornaro Piscopia, Maria Gaetana Agnesi, and Laura Bassi. Some were married, some were nuns, some were single. The last one, the eighteenth-century physicist Laura Bassi, was the first woman ever to earn a university chair in a scientific field of study; she had the full support of Pope Benedict XIV. Laura Bassi earned her chair in physics at the university of Bologna, and to this day the number of women studying physics in Italy is greater than in any other Western country.

Recreation is over; time for vespers.

5 Vespers: faith

Lauds takes place at sunrise; vespers starts at sunset. With the sunrise comes the challenge of practicing in the real world the love and the freedom proclaimed and meditated upon during matins. Now, at vespers, the challenge of the day is over: what has been accomplished, usually less than expected, lies before one's eyes as does what has been left undone; there will be no more working hours until the sun rises again. It is the moment of faith.

In summer, when we begin vespers, the monastic church is still lit directly by the setting sun. In winter, it is rather dusky. We turn on the electric light and the Christ hanging above the altar again becomes four-armed in the window reflection, ready once more to embrace the world like it did at matins. The psalms are less upbeat than those of lauds, but the canticle bursts with inner joy. The canticle of vespers is the *Magnificat*, the hymn that Mary of Nazareth sang in the mountains of Judea after having given her conscious, free and fully personal assent to God's proposal: do you want to be pregnant from the Spirit and give birth to God? Mary answered yes.

Theology needs to be distinguished from philosophy. Philosophy starts with human experience and uses reason to try to make sense of it; theology also starts from human experience and uses reason to try to make sense of it, but the human experience from which theology originates is of a very peculiar kind: it is the experience of some people, like Mary, who claim to have experienced God. Traditional Christian theology does not try to prove that Mary became pregnant from God, or that God was indeed born in first-century Palestine, died on a cross, and was resurrected as a God three days after being executed as a criminal. Each one of these statements is baffling for reason in the sense that reason cannot contain it, but this does not imply that reason becomes annulled by faith. Faith is a human capacity to trust in that which reason cannot deduce or verify. Faith is not subordinate to reason but neither does it nullify it. Reason is necessary in order to critically assess the consequences of a particular faith and to hold it accountable to itself (by questioning its coherence) and to others (by probing its ethical or moral soundness). The existence or non-existence of God can be neither proved nor disproved rationally. Consequently, reason cannot prove or disprove any action or interaction performed by God.

My decision to enter the monastery was not motivated by a rational consideration of the different options open to me at that particular moment of my life. It was motivated by an inner experience that I considered and still consider an experience of God. I felt – without sound or vision – that Jesus was calling me to be a nun at the particular monastery where I was hosted for a few weeks in order to prepare for a medical exam. Is it possible that I confused my own psychological needs or desires with the voice of God? Yes, it is possible. How can I know for sure that I did not deceive myself? I cannot know for sure. Faith involves risk, an existential risk that can only be freely assumed. In 1995 I assumed responsibility for interpreting what I experienced as a call from God and for acting accordingly. Today, twenty years later, I assume responsibility for continuing to interpret what I experienced as a call from God and for acting accordingly.

Faith and freedom: the title and underlying topic of this book is often perceived as a contradiction, an either/or disjunctive. Having religious faith is identified with binding yourself to a power called God and granting this power authority to command you and control your life. The apocryphal Gospel of Judas, which became famous after having been published in 2006 by the National Geographic Society, exemplifies the tension between faith and freedom in a particularly poignant way. The gospels are documents written in the first two centuries of Christianity that explain the life and collect the sayings of Jesus of Nazareth. There are four gospels (Mark, Matthew, Luke, and John) considered canonical, i.e., that are accepted by traditional Christianity as being inspired by God, and more than fifteen that are thought of as "apocryphal," i.e., that are not accepted as canonical. The publication of the

Gospel of Judas coincided with the release of the film *The Da Vinci Code*, based on Dan Brown's 2003 best-selling novel. The non-specialized press fed directly into the controversy surrounding the book and the film by presenting the Gospel of Judas as an instance of suppressed truth resurfacing after almost 2000 years of ecclesiastical repression. Despite the marketing it received, the Gospel of Judas is no theological break-through; it is rather conventional and far less interesting or innovative than the four canonical gospels. It does, however, allow its readers to grasp at a deeper level something that the canonical gospels insinuate, but do not fully develop; namely, the depth of the puzzlement experienced by the first Christians at the idea of a God who does not control human behavior, a God not only effectively challenged but even historically defeated by human will.

The Gospel of Judas is named after the disciple that the canonical gospels identify as Jesus' betrayer, the one who handed him over to the Roman soldiers in exchange for thirty pieces of silver paid to him by the chief priests. The canonical Gospel of Mark, allegedly the earliest to be written, is as usual the most succinct: "And

Judas Iscariot, one of the twelve, went unto the chief priests, to betray him unto them" (Mark 14:10). Reading this straightforward sentence, one gets the impression that Judas made the decision out of his own free will; later in the Gospel it becomes clear that Judas goes through with his decision up to the end, and that the consequence is the arrest, torture, and execution of Jesus. The Gospel of Matthew elaborates further: "And he [Jesus] answered and said, 'He that dips his hand with me in the dish, the same shall betray me. The Son of man goes as it is written of him: but woe unto that man by whom the Son of man is betrayed! It would have been good for that man if he had not been born.' Then Judas, which betrayed him, answered and said, 'Master, is it I?' He said unto him, 'Thou hast said'" (Matthew 26:23–6). Matthew, like Mark, implies that Judas makes the decision on his own, but the sentence "The Son of man goes as it is written of him" introduces the theme of scriptural predestination: things do not happen in the world, and particularly to Jesus, without God having predicted them. One could say that Matthew reasserts divine prerogatives in the face of history gone awry. The Gospel of Luke strengthens this same idea: "But, behold, the hand of him that betrays me is with me on the table. And truly the Son of man goes, as it was determined: but woe unto that man by whom he is betrayed!" (Luke 22:21–2). Luke uses the stronger expression "as it was determined" instead of "as it is written," and introduces the theme of "Satan" in his description of Judas' decision to betray Jesus: "Then entered Satan into Judas surnamed Iscariot, being of the number of the twelve. And he went his way, and communed with the chief priests and captains, how he might betray him unto them" (Luke 22:3–4). The way Luke describes the betrayal (Judas does what Satan makes him to do; what happens to Jesus was predetermined) seems to reduce human agency and free will practically to zero. The Gospel of John agrees with Luke on the topic of Satan or "the devil": "And supper being ended, the devil had now put into the heart of Judas Iscariot, Simon's son, to betray him" (John 13:2). Then John makes a disquieting move: he links Judas' final resolution to betray Jesus to something that Jesus himself does to Judas: "Jesus answered, 'He it is [the betrayer], to whom I shall give a sop, when I have dipped it.' And when he had dipped the sop, he gave it to Judas Iscariot, the son of Simon. And after the sop Satan entered into him. Then said Jesus unto him, 'What you do, do quickly' " (John 13:26–7). The way John describes the sequence of events during the Last Supper places Jesus in a commanding position and makes Judas *almost* into Jesus' instrument.

The disquieting idea that Judas the betrayer, instead of being a human being exercising his free will in opposition to God's plans, might indeed be no more than an instrument in the hands of an Almighty God who has no respect for human agency is totally absent in Mark, starts to develop in Matthew and Luke, and seems to come to almost full expression in John. In the apocryphal Gospel of Judas, this disquieting idea takes an unexpected turn: after having identified him as his most enlightened disciple, Jesus explicitly commissions Judas to betray him: "But you will exceed all of them. For you will sacrifice the man that clothes me." The expression "the man that clothes me" never appears in the canonical gospels. The canonical gospels take the Incarnation (the fact that God became truly human) at face value, while in the Gospel of

93

Judas Jesus is not truly human but only *appears* to be so; he is not really human and he is not really betrayed either, because he himself commands Judas to hand him over to the Romans. In the Gospel of Judas, Jesus (God) remains in control and rewards Judas as his closest collaborator: " 'Look, you have been told everything. Lift up your eyes and look at the cloud and the light within it and the stars surrounding it. The star that leads the way is your star.' Judas lifted up his eyes and saw the luminous cloud, and he entered it."

The Gospel of Judas presents the execution of Jesus as "a sacrifice to God." This idea is absent in the canonical gospels, but was later developed by certain medieval theologians and has been influential to this day. According to this view, God, despite the Incarnation, remains above historical circumstances and in control of them. The canonical gospels, on the contrary, show a God who becomes truly (and not only apparently) vulnerable, a God who is contradicted by the events that occur, a God that can be ignored and abandoned, a God that can be truly (and not only apparently) betrayed and killed. The canonical gospels show a God ready to love freely in the direst of circumstances; a God who has made us in Her image so that we too can remain ready to love in the direst circumstances, if we freely so choose. I believe that we are all, professed Christians or not, aware that regardless of the external circumstances of our life, there always remains in us the possibility of performing a genuine act – no matter how small, secret, or unexpected – of free love. Such is my faith.

The discovery of a God able to create and to honor human freedom to its ultimate ends led the thirteenth-century German theologian Gertrude of Helfta, together with her monastic sisters, to develop an alternative to the hegemonic Christology of the High Middle Ages. The dominant theology depicted Christ Jesus as the Pantocrator, God Almighty, King of the World. This image emphasized Christ's power to rule and to impose His Law on all creatures. He was conceived in the image and likeness of an Emperor, a commanding and sovereign Lord exercising His supreme authority from above. In the context of such a dominant view, it is surprising that in Gertrude's first experience of God, Jesus appears to her as a young boy of sixteen with no majestic attributes. At the time of this experience Gertrude was a mature nun of twenty-six who had been living in the monastery since the age of five. From that first experience onwards, Gertrude's understanding of Jesus grows ever more intimate, and she starts to develop the idea of God's vulnerability without abandoning the idea of God's majesty or God's transcendence. It is precisely the simultaneity of God's transcendence and God's vulnerability that becomes the central tenet of Gertrude's theology.

In order to grasp adequately this aspect of Gertrude's theology, it is particularly revealing to compare the inner experience she describes in chapter VIII of her book *The Herald of Divine Love* with the one described in chapter XIV. On both occasions, Gertrude is participating in the mass of Sunday XV in the ordinary liturgical time. On both occasions, the experience takes place after chanting the antiphon of the day: "Be my protector." In her first experience Jesus offers his heart to her as a promised land where she can find rest and protection: "Touching during the recitation of these verses your blessed chest with your venerable hand, you showed me which one was the land that your endless liberality was promising me." In her second experience, the roles are surprisingly reversed and Jesus is the one looking for comfort and rest in Gertrude's heart: "You made me understand by the words of this introit, only Object of my love, that, being wearied by the persecutions and outrages that so many people inflict on you, you looked for my heart, that you might repose therein. Therefore, each time that I entered therein during these three days, you appeared to me as if lying down there like a person exhausted by extreme languor." The experience of God's vulnerability and need is possible for Gertrude because of the Incarnation, that most distinctive and peculiar of all Christian claims: God took flesh, existing as a human being in time and space in all God's plenitude. In early Christianity, this idea seemed plainly absurd to those who were wise; and to those who were religious it seemed outrageous. It is likely that this continues to be the case today. The idea of God does not agree well with the idea of limit. And yet, the spatial and temporal limits imposed on us are in fact never obstacles to the realization of our potential for love (our divine potential) in all its fullness. These limits are indeed the condition of possibility for our freedom in the same way that air is the condition of possibility for Kant's dove: "The light dove, cleaving the air in her free flight, and feeling its resistance, might imagine that its flight would be still easier in empty space," wrote Kant in the introduction to his *Critique of Pure Reason*.

Trust, freedom, joy, depth, intimacy, body, serenity, light, repose, kiss, and sweetness are some of the words that keep reappearing in Gertrude's writings. They express how she experienced God and how she talked about God to the many pilgrims who queued at the door of the monastery to talk to her and to her sisters. The theological circle of Helfta is responsible for having started the tradition of the "sacred heart" of Jesus, duly understood not as a kitsch depiction of superficial sweetness, but as a serious response to God's invitation to friendship and personal intimacy. Gertrude left behind her childish quest for an almighty controlling God in order to discover a God who was indeed vulnerable, and who was expecting *and actually needing* from her the unique and original act of love that only she could perform and that needs to be constantly renewed. Gertrude discovered that God expected such a personal relationship of love from her, as God expects from each of us. The striking combination of God's majesty and God's vulnerability is the theological *novum* introduced by the nuns of Helfta, a *novum* that reflects the gospel at its purest. Gertrude illustrated this double dimension of the unique love of God with the image of the heart and the two rays of light: golden for the divinity, rose for the flesh of the Incarnation. In the Incarnation, God has undergone what all classical notions of God most abhor, that is, *change*. God has changed, has acquired a body that, through the Resurrection, has been incorporated into God's self for all eternity.

The nuns of Helfta did talk to each other about these inner experiences and did help each other to take seriously the challenges they involved, but each of them was utterly alone when facing them. In the process, they were discovering the depths of what modern thought calls "subjectivity"; they were true thirteenth-century pioneers of the discovery of subjectivity and individual freedom; they anticipated the *devotio moderna* and were transformed by their experience in a way that gave them the authority to inspire others on the path to personal fulfill-ment and joy. They are an example of female leadership that escaped patriarchal control and developed in a seemingly natural and daring way.

Another pioneer in exploring subjectivity and individual freedom in depth was the seventeenth-century Spanish nun and theologian María Jesús de Ágreda. She argued that the maternity of Mary of Nazareth, proclaimed "mother of God" by the Christian tradition, was the theological locus of human freedom. Her approach can be most succinctly expressed by stating that the goal of human life is to "bring to light the Light," the Light with a capital "L" being God and the expression "to bring to light" being taken in the sense it can have in Spanish: *to give birth* (*dar a luz*). The goal of human life is "to bring to light the Light," to give birth to God, to become "a mother of God." The expression "mother of God" is a translation of the Greek *Theotokos*, which literally translates as "the one who gives birth to God." So this is the idea: God can only exist in space and time if "born" from a human being, that is, if a human being freely accepts – as Mary of Nazareth did – to conceive and to give birth to God. The Christian tradition claims that approximately 2000 years ago this happened literally, biologically, through Mary of Nazareth and that, as a consequence, God was physically conceived and born as a human being and then lived for around thirty-three years before being executed by the State as a criminal. It is an astonishing claim that theology takes at face value and whose consequences it then proceeds to analyze. For María Jesús de Ágreda, the main consequence is an immediate validation of human freedom: God could not have become human without the free assent of Mary of Nazareth.

De Ágreda devotes a few pages of her book *The Mystical City of God* (1660) to describing how Mary reacts to God's request, how she listens, how she assesses critically what she has heard and poses her question: "How shall this be, seeing I know not a man?" And then, to how she dwells in herself and takes her time to ponder the proposal and its possible consequences. According to the Gospel of Luke, Mary finally answers: "Behold the handmaid of the Lord; be it unto me [*fiat mihi*] according to thy word." De Ágreda analyzes this answer and wonders which *word of God* it is that Mary is ready to let be unto her. Inspired by the opening sentence of the Gospel of John, "In the beginning was the Word," de Ágreda refers Mary's *fiat* to the first word that God pronounces in the Bible: *fiat lux* (let there be light). These are the words pronounced by God in the book of Genesis on the first day of Creation. What "light" is it that God is talking about? God cannot refer to the light of the sun because the sun is not created until the fourth day. The light of the first day of Creation that brings cosmos out of chaos is no other than the Logos (the Word), conceived as the "principle of intelligibility" of the world; it is the light of enlightenment, of comprehension and understanding, of making sense. The Logos-Word that existed from the beginning as the second person of the Trinity becomes the principle of intelligibility of Creation when God contracts (*tzimtzum*) in order to make room for us (*perichoresis*). The existence of the second person of the Trinity implies that in God there is diversity: there is in God from all eternity a truly "other" of the Father that is the "condition of possibility" for the historical existence of the world as truly "other" than God.

In the beginning of Creation God declares: *fiat lux*. At a given moment in history, Mary declares:

fiat mihi... and in so doing she "brings to light the Light." Only then is Creation completed, when the Logos-Light is present in it not only as its "principle of intelligibility" but as the Logos really is: as a person. The divine person becomes historical and reveals to the world the fullness of God's free (gracious) love. In the *fiat* of Mary of Nazareth, Creation finds its fulfillment.

Our goal as persons made in the image of God is none other than to "bring to light the Light." The Logos cannot exist in the world without us. The maternity of Mary is unique and extraordinary in its historicity because only she has given birth to God in the flesh. Nonetheless, Incarnation and Redemption only reach their goal when each of us freely disposes ourselves, as Mary did, for a loving dialogue with God that will leave us metaphorically pregnant. This dialogue need not be explicitly Christian or even religious: according to the first letter of John, *where there is love, there is God*. Opening oneself to personal love is necessary in order to find meaning in life; personal love (loving somebody who is free to say no to you) is the Light with a capital "L", the principle of intelligibility without which the world makes no sense.

Each chapter of de Ágreda's book ends with an intervention by Mary of Nazareth that not only ratifies what the author has argued in the chapter, but also introduces some corrections and modifications. At the end of the chapter where de Ágreda explains Mary's *fiat*, Mary herself declares:

> *My daughter, I see you are admired, and with reason, for having known with a new light the mystery of God's humbleness in uniting with the human nature in the womb of a poor maiden as I was. But now I want you to turn your attention to yourself and ponder that God's humbleness was not to favor me alone, but to favor you as much as me. The Lord's Mercy knows no end and He enjoys and takes care of each person who cares to welcome Him as if that person were the only existing creature in the world and if only for her He had become man. Hence, thank with all the strength of your affection the coming of the Lord to the world as if you were alone in it; and then thank Him afterwards because He came exactly in that personal way for each one. And if you understand and confess with vivid faith that*

God Himself, infinite in attributes and eternal in majesty, is the one who came to me and took human flesh in my entrails, then you have to understand and confess as well that the same God is looking for you, calling you, taking care of you, caressing you and turning Himself fully to you, as if you were God's only creature; ponder well and consider what responsibility that entails and turn your understanding into vivid acts of faith and love, for all has been given to you by such a King and Lord that came to you when you could not search for God nor reach God. (*The Mystical City of God*, Pt 2, Bk III, ch. 11, para. 141)

The summit of Creation started in Mary of Nazareth, but it is still unfinished. It will only be completed when each of us acts like her and expresses from the most intimate center of our freedom the *fiat* that brings to light the Light.

It is dark in the monastic church. After vespers comes the time for personal prayer we call "lectio"; it lasts one hour and a half.

6   Compline: forgiveness

In some monasteries, the prayer of compline is conducted almost totally in the dark, with only a candle burning at the feet of an image of Mary and the monks or nuns reciting the psalms by heart. Our church is illuminated during compline, but we keep it almost dark for the preceding half hour, so that nuns and guests can sit there in quiet. A single light focuses on the Christ of the window, creating a soothing atmosphere. I feel invited every night to take a distance from whatever has worried or occupied me during the day, to acknowledge that my strength is limited and that I need rest. I remind myself of the words that Pope John XXIII allegedly addressed every night to Jesus: "I need to sleep now; you take over!" Time to learn to let go, to relax, to rest.

Often, letting go is not possible because there is something pending; something unresolved that causes guilt or invites judgment. This is why the prayer of compline starts with an invitation to review one's actions, thoughts, and omissions during the day and to ask for forgiveness for all one's shortcomings. On weekdays, asking for forgiveness is done with a collective prayer and each keeps to herself whatever it is that she concretely considers to have been her shortcomings for the day. But on feast days we have the opportunity to ask for forgiveness in a more personal way, because instead of holding the prayer in the church we hold it in our recreation room and there are no guests. However, there is no obligation to speak; in fact, the Rule of Benedict explicitly advises not to make public intimate shortcomings that do not affect others. What is encouraged is a willingness to acknowledge and ask for forgiveness for attitudes that have been public and notorious (shouting, for instance, or being careless and breaking something, or arriving late to prayer or meals, or forgetting one's responsibilities with obvious consequences for others).

When I entered the monastery, I noticed that one of the sisters would unfailingly speak up at compline on all feast days, and would always say the same thing: "I am sorry that I..." The content of her self-accusation is not what matters; what matters is that she never failed to repeat the same shortcoming week after week. After six months or so, I started to become nervous, thinking that somebody should help her get over this, do something about it, solve it! Now, almost twenty years later, this sister is ninety-eight years old and does not usually join the community for compline, but while she did, I heard her, week after week and year after year, unfailingly acknowledging the same shortcoming. After a few years, instead of getting nervous about it, I began to realize two things: firstly, that while improving one's character is always desirable, it is often not possible, particularly past a certain age; secondly, that there is something more important for community life than getting rid of one's imperfections, namely, acknowledging them.

It is my experience that having life-mates who acknowledge their imperfections brings a very kind and deep type of joy to one's life; the responsible acceptance of one's own faults widens life and activates the best part of oneself. I am not talking about self-justification or a "this is the way I am" attitude; the sister I mentioned was not at all defensive about her particular shortcoming; this is what puzzled me for a long while: that she was able to acknowledge her repeated failure calmly and seriously. She was indeed in a very concrete way able to take responsibility, over and over again, unfailingly, for herself, for her actions, her thoughts and her omissions. She was not perfect; she was free. She was able to accept herself without distorting her own image or having to pretend that she was better than she really was; she was able to forgive herself, and this is why in her company others could find the space to be themselves.

Taking responsibility for one's life is the most concise definition of personal freedom. It can also be called human maturity or full subjectivity. While writing my doctoral dissertation on the notion of "person" in classical Trinitarian theology in relation to the modern notion of "freedom" as self-determination, I came across Jacques Lacan's critique of the Christian notion of "person." Lacan rejected the notion for being substantial and ontological, for pretending to give concrete "content" to what a human being is or ought to be. To such a metaphysical notion of "person" the French psychoanalyst opposed the historical notion of "subject," understood as "an event," a happening in time that cannot be captured or predicted, a free and always surprising actualization of a subjective potential that needs to be constantly renewed. My own study of the notion of personhood in classical Trinitarian theology revealed Lacan's critique of the person to be historically inadequate, for Trinitarian personhood in its classical definition can by no means be conceived as lacking dynamism or historicity. In 2006, after I delivered a public lecture presenting my critique of Lacan's disregard for the classical notion of "person," a Spanish priest who had been Lacan's disciple informed me that at Lacan's funeral, Lacan's brother, who was a Benedictine monk and a priest, gave a homily linking Lacan's work on subjectivity to the Trinitarian notion of person. The Spanish priest had attended the funeral and had a copy of the homily that he later kindly sent me.

Both Lacan's subject and the Christian person are defined by the potential to break the causal chain, to escape determinism in order to initiate something new and unexpected. Lacan calls the actualization of this potential a "precipitation of subjectivity"; the Trinitarian tradition calls it a coherence between "essence" and "existence." And here comes the confusion: how can "actualizing one's essence" amount to "determining oneself"? Whoever or whatever has given an "essence" to my "being a person" has determined me; this is why the Lacanian subject, in order to be truly free, refuses to acknowledge any "personal essence" and speaks simply of an empty interiority, a potentiality with no metaphysical essence limited nevertheless by the concrete circumstances of one's upbringing. The concrete circumstances of my upbringing are what, according to Lacan, I must embrace in order to precipitate my subjectivity and be free. Some of those circumstances might be negative (e.g., learning to fear intimacy or learning abuse), others might be positive (e.g., being loved), but all of them are concrete and limited and cannot be taken as a norm. The universe of one's childhood needs to give way to new experiences in adolescence, but the process of becoming an adult never reaches full subjectivity once and for all; full subjectivity needs to be re-enacted repeatedly, over and against all conditionings, particularly those of our childhood. The attempt to eliminate most of our conditionings is futile. Our early experiences will accompany us all our life; we cannot get rid of them, but we (like the sister who always spoke at compline) can choose to take full responsibility for them. The moment we do so, we become free. The moment we stop doing so, we are bound again, determined, conditioned.

Lacan describes two basic modalities of trying to elude one's personal freedom: "alienation" and "separation." *Alienation* is the subjective experience of childhood: placing oneself under the guidance of someone else, acknowledging someone else's authority over oneself. *Separation* is the subjective experience of adolescence: asserting oneself as an autonomous being. What Lacan finds missing in separation is an acknowledgment of one's psychological conditionings. The adolescent rejects parental authority without realizing that she has internalized its demands. There is no "authentic personal core" that can sustain an autonomous self; autonomy is an illusion, a fantasy. What we call our "self" is a historical and arbitrary combination of the conditionings that happened to affect us in childhood: identifying with that set of conditionings and claiming it as one's separated or autonomous self amounts to self-deception: separation, instead of breaking the causal chain as true freedom does, only reinforces it. In order to truly break the causal chain one needs to *traverse the fundamental fantasy*, the fantasy of identifying with the set of conditionings that happened to affect us during our upbringing and shaped our character, that gave us a sense of personal identity and allowed us to assert ourselves as autonomous beings. Traversing the fundamental fantasy cannot be done in the abstract and cannot be done once and for all. It is a life's task. It amounts to taking full and continuous responsibility – like the monastic sister did – for one's particular conditionings, without confusing them with one's authenticity, but rather carrying them as an actively and consciously accepted burden; in the Christian language, it amounts to carrying one's cross. This is freedom.

The three main characters in Jesus' parable of the prodigal son (Luke 15:11–32) exemplify the three different existential answers to subjective freedom described by Lacan: alienation, separation, and traversing a fundamental fantasy. These three characters are a father and his two sons. The action starts when the younger son asks for his inheritance so that he can establish himself independently of his father; if the older son had also claimed his inheritance then the father would have been left with no means of survival; but the older son does not follow his brother's lead, instead remaining faithfully by the father. The younger son's quest for independence soon proves a failure: he is unable to sustain himself autonomously. When he finally returns in disgrace to the paternal house, the true message of Jesus' parable begins: the father welcomes the younger son with open arms; but the older son, the faithful son, is unable to accept his brother, unable to forgive him. Full of resentment, he shouts at the father: "Listen! For all these years I have been working like a slave for you, and I have never disobeyed your command; yet you have never given me even a young goat so that I might celebrate with my friends. But when this son of yours came back, who has devoured your property with prostitutes, you killed the fatted calf for him!"

The older son is *alienated*. He has alienated his freedom under his father's authority; he has remained with his father not out of love, but because he has not dared to leave like his younger brother did. The younger son is *separated*, he tried to thrive by neglecting his responsibility to his father, but expected his father to fulfill his responsibility to him even at the expense of his own livelihood (by gifting him his inheritance early). And the father? What is the subjective existential position of the father vis-à-vis his two sons? To his older son's recriminations, the father answers: "Son, you are always with me, and all that is mine is yours." The father does not claim any paternal authority over his son: he treats him as an equal. The father is free and expects his sons to be free. The older son, however, needs "the Law"; he needs an objective set of norms to regulate his freedom and contain his existential anguish. When the Law is broken, he expects punishment. He cannot accept that his younger brother, the one who broke the Law, should be rewarded. For his part, the younger son has broken with "the Law" (Jewish law required that grown-up children take care of their parents) and has tried to live without taking into account anything other than his own will and his own liking: "he traveled to a distant country, and there he squandered his property in dissolute living." He has lived an illusion of freedom. In contrast with both his sons, the father of the parable is free because he is able to act beyond his interests without alienating himself, without expecting payment or an external reward for it. The father acts beyond his interests knowingly and lovingly. Freely. He asserts himself without having to actualize any pre-existing "authentic self" that limits his capacity for action. His "authentic self" is the one that is created by his free loving action. There is no other authenticity. All the rest are internalized conditionings.

The father in the parable stands for God, in whose image and likeness all human beings have been created according to the biblical Genesis. The thirteenth-century theologian Thomas Aquinas interpreted the biblical expression "created in the image and likeness of God" according to the Aristotelian philosophical categories of "potentiality" and "actuality": the "image" is our potentiality for free (non-alienated) love; the "likeness" is the actuality of this potentiality; the actuality (our being *like*

God) takes place each time we realize a concrete action of free (non-alienated) love. The image is our *essence* (to be free and loving); the concrete actions that we undertake are our *existence*, and they can agree or not with our essence; only when our existence (what we concretely do) agrees with our essence are we free. So Lacan is right to point out that the Christian notion of person is essentialist, ontological, or metaphysical; but he misses the point when he opposes this essentialist notion of person to the historical notion of subject, because – as we have just seen – the "essence" of the Christian person as defined by Aquinas needs to actualize itself in history as "existence," and it can only do so when the person is ready to take responsibility in a non-alienated way, freely, for the concrete conditions of her life, like the father in the parable does. In Lacanian terminology, this amounts to traversing the fundamental fantasy, that is, abandoning the illusion that somewhere within me lies an "authentic self" to which I am accountable. Like the persons of the Trinity, my "authentic self" (*esse in*) is relational (*esse ad*); my essence is relational; being is communion (*esse cum*). Speaking of a "relational essence" amounts to blowing up the metaphysical essentialist construct. The "autonomous self" is an illusion, but personal freedom is not an illusion because there exists for each person the possibility of freely self-actualizing her potential for love. In this sense, both the Christian person and the Lacanian subject are called to "create themselves" out of nothing. For the Christian, this "nothing" is the empty space that God's contraction (*tzimtzum*) has lovingly opened up for us.

In Jesus' parable, both sons take action against their *essence*: the younger because he is not loving; the older because he is not free. What allows both of them a second chance is the forgiveness of their father: the father forgives the younger son's lack of love (the younger son abandoned the father and by requesting the inheritance effectively undermined his livelihood) and forgives as well the older son's lack of freedom (the older son remained with the father out of fear; he behaved towards him not as a son but as a slave). In reality, as Lacan's analysis of human subjectivization shows, both sons are lacking in love *and* freedom. Freedom and love are inseparable. By ignoring his obligations to his father and treating him badly, the younger son pursues an empty notion of the autonomous self. Instead of being free, he submits himself to his inner promptings without realizing that they are the result of his upbringing and his external conditions. Instead of freedom, he finds alienation. Thus does the parable describe the condition of the younger son after he has spent his father's money: "He would gladly have filled himself with the pods that the pigs were eating; and no one gave him anything." For a Jew who considers the pig an unclean animal and refuses to eat it, wishing to eat what the pigs eat is a metaphor for having fallen below the human condition. Meanwhile, by not daring to confront his father and tell him of his desire to have a feast with his friends, the older son is also lacking in love: love for himself, love for his father. The older son treats the father as a master, not as a friend; he doesn't love him, he fears him. That is why he cannot understand his father's words when the father says to him: "Son, you are always with me, and all that is mine is yours."

Forgiveness of self and others is what allows us to be free in our concrete life. The father in the parable had nothing to forgive himself but had a lot to forgive his sons. He is loving and free. We are not told whether the sons become loving and free. The younger son who wanted to be autonomous might now stay at the father's house out of fear, and the older son who didn't dare to be autonomous might now leave the father's house out of rage. We are not told whether they become loving and free, but we know that their father's forgiveness gives them a chance. And we also know that this chance is no guarantee for the future. It might happen that both sons are moved by the love of the father and react freely and lovingly to it, but only for a while. After a few months, the younger son might mistreat him again and the older son might repress himself again. Traversing one's own fundamental fantasy, achieving full subjectivation, is not a "state of being"; it is a historical reality that needs to be actualized over and over again. In biblical language: the human being is a pilgrim on earth (*homo viator / mulier viatora*).

Another of Jesus' parables (Matthew 18:23–35) vividly illustrates the fact that the experience of being forgiven does not necessarily imply a personal transformation towards freedom and love. Jesus tells of a king who wishes to settle his accounts and decides to send one of his servants to prison together with his whole family until he pays back all that he owes the king; the servant begs the king's pardon and obtains it. The servant's debt was 10,000 talents and all of it is forgiven to him. On exiting the king's presence, he finds a fellow servant who owes him 100 denarii. The denarius was the accepted salary for a day's work by a common laborer. One talent equaled 6,000 denarii. Ten thousand talents amounted to 60 million denarii. The slave who has been forgiven 60 million, instead of forgiving his fellow slave who owes him only 100, reacts brutally against him: "seizing him by the throat, he said, 'Pay what you owe.' Then his fellow servant fell down and pleaded with him, 'Have patience with me, and I will pay you.' " The second servant uses the very same words that the first servant had used on pleading for mercy from the king. "But he refused; then he [the first servant] went and threw him [the second servant] into prison until he would pay the debt."

I have a personal experience that reveals the same dynamic that Jesus criticizes in this parable. It happened in my mid-twenties while praying according to the indications of Ignatius of Loyola, the founder of the Jesuits. In his spiritual exercises, Ignatius recommends using one's imagination to mentally reproduce one of the scenes described in the gospel as vividly as possible and then to include oneself in it as a character and observe what happens: what feelings, what actions, what thoughts are elicited by this exercise. I imagined the scene of the washing of the feet: Jesus washes the feet of his disciples at their last supper. Washing the feet was a task performed by slaves. I imagined myself as one of the disciples and I imagined Jesus kneeling in front of me, taking my foot and washing it. I felt unworthy of such treatment and filled with humbleness and gratitude. But then, the action (in my imagination) took an unexpected turn: Jesus rose up and moved on to the next disciple and – surprise! – he was somebody with whom I was deeply at odds at the moment; I came immediately out of my beatific meditative state to scold Jesus for making a mistake: *Not him! You can't kneel in front of him and wash his feet!*

From my mid-twenties to today, I have had plenty of opportunities to realize the central role of forgiveness in leading a loving and free life, and my shortcomings in relation to it. This is why in 2010, when requested by a Spanish magazine to answer the question "in what do you believe?" in less than 300 words, I wrote the following text:

IN WHAT I BELIEVE

I believe, above all, in forgiveness. I believe that our capacity for forgiveness reveals the bare truth of our capacity to love, and I am often surprised to encounter this capacity in people I don't particularly admire and to find it lacking in others I love dearly. More than once I have been surprised by my own difficulties with forgiving, and I have experienced the miracle of being forgiven. It is like being born again. Being born from love. The gospel tells us that the sinful woman showed great love because so much had been forgiven to her (Luke 7:47). It also warns us that even a person to whom much has been forgiven can treat others meanly and mercilessly (Matthew 18:23–35). And this is the second part of what I believe: I believe in freedom; I believe in the breaking of the causal chain that opens the world to poetry but also introduces the possibility of the most unjust arbitrariness. I believe that forgiveness is the greatest act of freedom. This means that everything can be forgiven but nobody can be compelled to forgive. Forgiveness cannot be forced and its outcome cannot be predicted. The woman who forgives her husband for abusing her can decide, even as she forgives him, that they should not go on living together. God alone can judge the authenticity and the scope of an act of forgiveness. Forgiveness is the most rational of all acts, because it recognizes that something more than automatism rules the world. Forgiveness is the act that allows us to be creators, like God; the act that allows us to start over once again; seventy times seven (Matthew 18:22). (El Ciervo, no. 716, November 2010)

We have been created free. This is why we can always break the causal chain with an unexpected word or action. Forgiveness is the fullest expression of freedom. In the words of Francis of Assisi: *where there is hatred, let me sow love.* The Spanish mystic John of the Cross put it even more succinctly: *where there is no love, put love.*

Compline is over. Time to rest.